# Focus: The Railroad in Transition

# Focus:
## The Railroad in Transition

**Robert S. Carper**

South Brunswick and New York: A. S. Barnes and Company
London: Thomas Yoseloff Ltd

A. S. Barnes and Co., Inc.
Cranbury, New Jersey 08512

Thomas Yoseloff Ltd
18 Charing Cross Road,
London W.C. 2, England

6678
Printed in the United States of America

To Pamela and Bruce, into whose vocabulary
the term "choo-choo train" has never entered.

# Acknowledgments

I would like to thank the following people and organizations for their wholehearted cooperation and work in making *Focus: The Railroad in Transition* a reality:

Mr. F. H. Woolfall and Mr. H. D. Talkington of the New York Central; Mr. W. E. Baird and Mr. R. A. Rutledge of the Pennsylvania Railroad — and especially Mr. Paul Lotz, Safety Supervisor of the Pennsylvania's Conway Yards, without whose aid many of the photographs taken there could not have been possible.

I would also like to thank each of the following contributors of photographs and technical data that enabled the scope of the book to reach far beyond the lens of my own camera:

Mr. James A. Van Sant of General Steel Industries; Mr. D. F. Given of United Aircraft Corporate Systems Center; Mr. D. Gregg Cummings of Electro-Motive Division of General Motors Corporation; Mr. Hiroshi Hattori of the Japanese National Railways; Mr. Jacques J. Mennier of the French National Railroads; Mr. D. W. Pazdur of General American Transportation Corporation, and Mr. Elliott Gordon of ACF Industries, Inc.

Also, Mr. Carl Sundberg, president of Sundberg-Ferar, Inc. and Mr. Kenneth Drake of Kenneth Drake Associates for photographs and data of the auto-on-train project; Mr. Alan D. Barber of the Aluminum Company of America, Inc.; Mr. Alex C. Wylie of the News Bureau of General Electric Company; and Mrs. Priscilla R. Crane, Director of Public Information for the office of High-Speed Ground Transportation.

Last but not least, there is a special bouquet of thanks to a young lady by the name of Mrs. Fern Carper who typed all the text and captions for the manuscript, helped in the layout, did proofreading, handled the big volume of correspondence, and many other tasks necessary to pull the manuscript together, all in addition to her normal duties of keeping the household running as wife and mother.

ROBERT S. CARPER
Pittsburgh, Pennsylvania

# Contents

# Introduction

Take a map. Locate Chicago, the focal point of our nation's transportation system. Now draw a line southward to St. Louis, the second-largest transportation center. Swing an arc eastward through Louisville and over to Washington. Now draw an arc over the ocean northeastward to Boston. Finally, swing an arc westward over Lake Ontario, across the midsection of Michigan, and back to Chicago.

You have just drawn the Northeast Quadrant of the United States. It is here where the heaviest industrial concentration of the free world is centered. It is here where the heaviest population concentration of the United States is located. It is here where the commerce generated by this huge industrial complex must be transported. And it is here where the inhabitants of these huge metropolitan centers must travel back and forth, among and between these giant cities.

It is here that within the twenty-year span from 1947 to the present the railroads have passed through the most remarkable transition in their entire history. By their own hand, unaided by any subsidy, they have cast out a traditional form of motive power which had been a legend in its own time for a radically new form of locomotive, saving untold millions of dollars. The railroads followed this up by rallying in the face of an almost bizarre picture of subsidized competition to introduce a whole host of subsequent technological changes to maintain their entity as privately-owned common carriers of the nation's goods. At the same time, the railroads experienced through this same subsidized competition as well as their own shortcomings the almost instantaneous shakedown of their passenger-carrying capability to where it is now at the point of rebound due to the resultant unbalance of our nation's overall transportation system in the face of unprecedented economic growth.

The camera has been unpacked from its bag, the film has been carefully loaded, and the lenses have been focused beside the steel tracks upon this overwhelming transition — from the last days of the Iron Horse to the 3000-horsepower low-profile diesel, the tri-level automobile rack car, the New Tokaido Line, and *TurboTrain*. Along with this, the story unfolds with words depicting how and why this has all come about, together with a portrayal of where it is now going.

Let us begin with the year 1947, the last full year of life of the Iron Horse. . . .

# 1

## The Death of the Iron Horse

Picture yourself walking along a small country road on a quiet summer day in August. The road winds its way across fields, through wooded patches, across a small creek, and then is abruptly sliced in two by four pairs of shimmering steel rails. A solitary white crossing-gate arm rises into the blue sky, marking the spot where the main line of a mighty railroad crosses the country lane. These rails, carrying the commerce of a nation, are seldom still, but on this lazy summer day, everything is quiet save for the sound of an occasional bird or cricket. The steel rails ripple in the heat waves rising from the hot afternoon sun. And then you hear it.

A low, melancholy wail in the distance breaks the quiet heat of the afternoon. Your walk is interrupted. Again you hear it; this time a little louder, a little less melancholy, a little more imperative. Along the horizon a thin whisp of black smoke rises. Now the whistle echoes a shrill warning, and a sharp staccato bark cleaves the once-still air. The rails pound to the approach of an oncoming freight train, with the Iron Horse at its head raising up clouds of black and white smoke, blasting the sky with its powerful exhaust, silver rods flashing in an oscillating rhythm, like some maddened monster racing against time itself. In a split second it roars by, with red, yellow, and black cars flashing by the lowered crossing gate. A gentle rain of cinders falls, the sulfurous odor of soft coal smoke lingers despite the rushing avalanche of boxcars clattering over the crossing. Soon that unique curiosity called the caboose heralds the end of the train, with the roar gradually subsiding to the quiet of the afternoon. The low wail of the whistle can be heard once again as the train no longer can be seen, and the last faint rumbling of the train disappears. You resume your walk, still awed by that wonderful machine of pure, unharnessed power which shattered the stillness of a clear, idyllic afternoon in the countryside.

Let your eye stretch down that expanse of steel rail, farther than it can see physically, far enough to reach the city, where the four-track main line becomes open expanses of railroad yards and terminals. Here there are no swaying fields of grass, no quiet wooded areas, no rippling waves of heat rising to meet the clear blue skies. For here, there are no clear blue skies. Here the commerce of a nation rests on its journey to its final destination sitting on long tracks nestled between block after block of dirty dilapidated houses and soot-filled patches of barren ground. Pigeons by the thousands swoop and dive to grow fat on the grain leaking out of boxcars, with equal numbers of unseen rats competing with them for it. Grimy urchins dart in and out of the cars standing still on the tracks, alert for the ever-present

13

railroad cop. Clouds and clouds of brown and black soft coal smoke blot out the miserable surroundings, churned skyward by snorting yard engines or bellowing road engines pushing and pulling the strings of cars through the yards twenty-four hours a day, seven days a week. Red, yellow, and green signal lights wink through the clouds of steam and smoke belching forth from these ironclad monsters. Aboard these black mechanical giants men peer into the roaring infernoes of their boilers, shovelling coal frantically to keep the fires burning ever hotter, then carefully observing water level gauges or steam pressure indicators or else looking out of the cab down the long rows of cars in the yards for signals, to call them over to the man who sits behind the throttle, on the other side of the cab. This man, the locomotive engineer, is as much a part of the snorting black beast as its clanging bell or its ear-piercing whistle. Clad in his blue pin-stripe overalls and red bandana around his neck, a wad of tobacco stuffed in his cheek and a solid gold watch chain offsetting the dirt and soot and grease on his overalls, the engineer looks down the track for the signal of green over red over red, slams the Johnson bar forward, leans back on the throttle, and hears the explosion of exhaust roaring into the smog-laden skies over the yards. Turning over the valve which blows sand against the huge wheels slipping for traction on the wet rail, he yells across to his fireman, "More steam, dammit!" And then the gates of Hell open again, the shovelling starts again, the cab rocks to and fro as the huge locomotive begins to blast forward, the smoke rises higher, ever higher, and the leaden gray skies become just a little blacker. It is incredible how the inhabitants of these wretched soot-begrimed dwellings near the railroad endure the incessant belching, puffing, clanging, and slamming of the Iron Horse against train after train with the cinders raining against their rotting roof shingles and the smoke crawling ever deeper into the innermost passages of their already blackened lungs. It is as if life itself has been brutally transformed into a world of Stygian darkness created by soft coal smoke, shutting off forever all traces of fresh air and daylight.

But somehow life manages to go on. It has to. For let there be no smoke and then there will be no jobs. The slum dweller has never had so much as a high school education and as a consequence no formal understanding of the laws of economics. But everything is gauged by the long pounding trains which storm by his rattling windows, be they the long freight trains or the dark green passenger limiteds. Let this commerce stop, and the whole world stops. And so it goes on, into the year 1947. In that year, the staccato of the exhaust of the Iron Horse, which had for over a century split the quiet of the countryside like thunder and had sent tons upon tons of smoke skyward to fall over the city in a steady black rain turned into its death rattle.

Death rattle? It was inconceivable that anything like the steam locomotive could ever die. Was it not the steam engine that was the mainspring of the Great Industrial Revolution that began in the mid-Nineteenth Century? Was it not in 1829 that the first crude boiler was mounted atop a rig attached to wheels which, wonder of wonders, could not only propel itself along a track of steel rails but could pull other carriages on wheels? Somebody during this period dubbed it the Iron Horse, and wasn't there all the similarity in the world behind the name? It could race across the countryside at breathtaking speeds with the most important of passenger trains or plod unerringly forward with wagonload strung up to wagonload of goods. It rested in its own peculiar kind of stable called the roundhouse when it was not working. Like its namesake, is required many attendants to service it and to attend to its every need between runs. Steamfitters, boilermakers, metalsmiths, and a whole host of other craftsmen kept it in the finest running condition and appearance. In the huge expanses of shops and roundhouses which marked the railroad scene, men worked day and night to tear apart the boilers, re-line them with new firebrick, and repair the miles and miles of tubing. Once repaired, other men stood atop these steaming monsters pouring sand into cylinder domes, filling the huge tenders with water more pure than humans accustom themselves to drink, and then pouring tons of coal into the vast holds of the tenders. Like the spirited Thoroughbred ready to run a race or the modest milk horse ready to go on his daily rounds or the rugged draft horse ready to pull the overloaded wagons, so emerged the swift passenger locomotive from the shops ready for the Limited, so emerged the rugged freight locomotive from the ready track for the long black string of coal-laden cars which had to go over the mountains. This was indeed the Iron Horse.

From its early astute beginning, the steam locomotive grew to become the living symbol of the American railroad. The railroad forged a trail across the Continent, quickly moving inland the civilization which was deposited on the shores of the New World. Whole cities sprang up along the thousands upon thousands of miles of ribbons of rail laid down in the mid-nineteenth century. New social patterns developed, catalyzed to a large degree by the railroad. Migrations developed from the country to the city as industries and new jobs opened up, aided by the new, cheap means of moving goods and people from place to place. Since the railroad had to cross rivers and mountains, new needs in construction opened up new concepts in engineering, and that science flourished under the expansion of the railroad. Similarly, the emerging network of railroads had a lasting impact upon business and government, perhaps one which would one day boomerang against the railroads. But always at the forefront of all areas where the emerging railroad impacted upon the growing American nation was its symbol, the steam locomotive. It personified the unchained power by which the railroad empires were growing in the nineteenth century. It represented the Machine Age which was at the crux of the Great Industrial Revolution. But most of all, it captured the imagination of the people in such a manner as to become a virtual legend in its own time. Not until the advent of the space rocket would another device made by man so dwell in the minds of all who would see it.

It seemed almost like life personified. It was a manifestation of man's atavistic awe of fire. It was a product of man's craftsmanship with iron. It filled the air with an uncommon noise. It reached for new frontiers just beyond the horizon, embodying the pioneer instincts of the new American. It was power, the power of a new nation, of a new people, of a new kind of growth, and of a new breed of businessman that wielded it. The steam locomotive was eulogized in the arts, in writing, and in song. Personages like Casey Jones and Kate Shelley became enshrined heroes.

The Iron Horse could, with one blast of its ear-piercing whistle, conquer time and space. The steam locomotive was a benevolent dragon, expelling clouds of steam and balls of fire while turning the empty countryside into clusters of new cities, vibrant with trade and commerce. And it was with all of this awe-inspiring power that the Iron Horse grew up, became more sophisticated in design as the newly emerging engineering technology was harnessed to designing not with art but with science a more powerful machine. Craftsmen became skilled

designers; foundrymen became devoted masters of the art of metalworking. A blend of technological development and skilled craftsmanship characterized the Iron Horse of the twentieth century. Out of the huge foundries of Baldwin Locomotive Works of Eddystone, American Locomotive Company of Schenectady, and Lima Locomotive Works of Lima, Ohio rolled these huge, new machines.

The steam locomotive was unique in that it was first and foremost an individual. No two designs were exactly alike. Each railroad exercised its own individual desires upon the locomotive foundries, and the resultant products were the symbols of the railroad on which it would operate. As an example, the Pennsylvania Railroad received its first locomotive in 1831 when the *John Bull* built by Robert Stephenson in England was delivered to the Camden and Amboy Railroad, which later became part of the larger Pennsylvania system. The roster of 7667 steam locomotives which the Pennsylvania carried in 1920 consisted completely of machines designed and built by the railroad either in its own shops or in the huge Eddystone foundries of Baldwin. The locomotives carried the unmistakable trademarks of the railroad — a stubby, fat boiler with a huge square firebox, and a long square tender atop which a doghouse sat, reserved for the head-end brakeman. All locomotives were built for power — for power was what was needed to enable the plush tuscan-red passenger limiteds and the long trains of coal and merchandise to cross the rugged ridges of the Allegheny Mountains.

The New York Central had no rugged mountains to cross. It was advertised proudly as the "Water Level Route." Stretching from the broad Midwestern plains to the shores of the Great Lakes and down through the valleys of the Mohawk and Hudson Rivers, there were no grades of any significance. As a result, every New York Central locomotive had the graceful lines of a whippet, designed by that railroad over three generations. Speed was their forte, and whether it be behind a 75-car train of merchandise freight or the plush *Twentieth Century Limited*, the Mohawk freight locomotives or Hudson passenger locomotives swept along the lake shores and down the Hudson Valley night and day, the living personification of a great railroad.

Each railroad willingly underwrote the development cost of each succeeding generation of new steam power, and why not? The railroad held a virtual monopoly over intercity transportation and could do as it well pleased in designing power for its own individual needs. The railroads of the early twentieth century were proud empires ruled by mighty railroad barons such as the Hills, the Vanderbilts, and the Van Sweringens. It was under such men that the mighty ornate palaces of railroadiana such as New York's Grand Central Station and Pennsylvania Station, Cleveland's Union Terminal, Buffalo's Central Terminal, and the "big five" of Chicago — LaSalle, Union, Grand Central, Illinois Central, and Dearborn — rose to their prominence in the lives and affairs of the cities they occupied. Plush trains daily left their portals for distant cities, behind the mighty monarchs of the rails such as the K-4 Pacifics, and the J-3 Hudsons that characterized these railroads. Similarly, the powerful freight locomotives which chugged and belched and clanged and scraped with the heavy tonnage loads along the Great Lakes and over the Alleghenies and across the broad Midwest bore the unmistakable trademark of the railroads which they served.

Not only was the steam locomotive an individual with respect to the railroads that directed every last detail in its building, but it was just as much a specialist with respect to the duties it was called upon to fulfill. There were short, fat stumpy yard engines which puffed and bellowed as they broke up old trains and made up the new trains in the vast tangle of classification yards. There were the slightly larger local freight engines that wheezed their daily ten-car trains along the thousands of miles of branch-lines. Every child in every small hamlet knew almost personally the engineer and fireman of the morning local as it went about its daily rounds. There were the mighty freight locomotives that sent their powerful exhaust of smoke and steam reaching to the very heavens as they thundered out of the yards with a freight bound for distant cities. There were the even-more-powerful articulated compounds which had two sets of drive wheels that strained and blasted their way over the mountains of Pennsylvania and West Virginia with coal from the mines to the lake and ocean port cities.

And there were the passenger locomotives that raced through day and night with the plush limiteds and the fast mail and express trains. They were not built for switching or for local freights or for long coal trains. Speed was their mission, and this they did well. On May 11, 1893, Engineer Charles Hogan opened the throttle wide on the venerable 999 of the New York Central and it responded with a speed record of 112½ miles per hour between Batavia, N. Y. and Buffalo. Since then, the Pacifics and the Hudsons and the Niagaras had raced by along that same railroad, not equalling the 999's record by any means, but certainly establishing performance records for sustained speeds of 75 to 85 miles per hour with 16- and 18-car limiteds. A classic scene of railroadiana occurred every afternoon along the shores of Lake Michigan as, side by side, the K-4 Pacifics of the Pennsylvania would race eastward against the J-2 and J-3 Hudsons of the New York Central.

So thus was the picture of the Iron Horse, on the railroads of America's Northeast on the day when, thousands of miles across the Atlantic, the legions of the German Army in coal-bucket helmets roared eastward across the Polish plain, while swarms of gull-winged dive bombers struck at the helpless cities of Poland. World War II had begun. An increasing measure of help which this country would provide to its free allies before becoming enmeshed in this war herself on a fateful Sunday in December 1941 began to show up on the railroads. The freight trains became longer and longer with food and increasingly larger amounts of strategic materials beginning to head for the port cities. And then, Pearl Harbor delivered to our railroads the greatest challenge they had ever been called upon to meet.

On December 7, 1941, the railroads had full steam up, ready to tackle this most formidable task. The job was to haul millions upon millions of tons of wartime commerce from the mines, from the mills, from the stamping plants and the assembly shops and the wheatfields and the farms to ships at sea. Behind the racing passenger locomotives rolled long trains stuffed with millions of men also headed for the ships at the port cities, ready to embark upon the most colossal war the United States was ever to fight in its history. Behind straining, groaning freight engines rolled guns and tanks, shells, food, jeeps, coal, and oil — all on their way to victory.

For five years the factories and draft boards produced their daily loads of material and men and fed them into the war machine. For five years the steam locomotive's whistle cut through the troubled air with a call to victory as it raced through the land by day and by night with its long cargoes of men and material. And then, with the blast of a mighty bomb, the holocaust was over.

The railroads were instrumental in America's

achievement of victory in World War II. Now they were ready to resume their peacetime roles as the ships returned to our shores with the men that had fought — and won. The foundries of American Locomotive, Baldwin, and Lima had embarked upon the building of the most refined and modern versions of the Iron Horse ever known. Committed to the building of tanks, guns, and steam locomotives by the War Production Board, their designers, masters of the craft of boiler and transmission design had turned out the masterful Berkshire which raced trains at 70 miles per hour along the shores of Lake Erie on the Nickel Plate Road, and were raced in turn by the Mohawks of the New York Central whose line paralleled it all the way from Cleveland to Buffalo. Over the Alleghenies came the 2–10–4 Decapods with the keystone blazer of the Pennsylvania. Across the cornfields of Illinois came the 4–8–4 Northerns with 60-mile-per hour banana trains all the way from New Orleans to Chicago.

The year was now 1947. With the reverberations of the diesel locomotive throbbing louder and louder, the Age of Steam was about to enter its finest hour.

There was the class S-1 Niagara of the New York Central. This locomotive was the railroad's attempt to combine the pulling power of the Mohawk freight locomotive with the speed of the classic Hudson. Weighing over 470,000 pounds on the rail, this locomotive was capable of pulling over 100 cars of merchandise freight or racing from Chicago to New York with the 20-car *Twentieth Century Limited* in sixteen hours, held back from an even better performance record by speed restrictions. Improved firing systems gave this locomotive only a faint gray exhaust as it raced along the Mohawk valley or along the Cleveland lakefront. Even to this day, this locomotive is venerated by the engineers who now pilot the mightiest diesels ever built along the Water Level Route.

The Pennsylvania, not to be outdone, produced a shark-nosed streamlined T-1 four-cylinder locomotive which raced westward from Harrisburg to Chicago and to St. Louis with the finest passenger trains on that line, such as the *Broadway Limited*, the *General*, the *Jeffersonian*, and the *Spirit of St. Louis*. With four pair of driving wheels, it was capable of climbing over the Alleghenies at speeds never before known and only rivalled before by K-4 Pacifics running doubleheaded. Once over the Alleghenies west of Pittsburgh, it could race along the plains of Ohio,

Indiana, and Illinois at 85–90 miles per hour.

The Pennsylvania also produced an experimental turbine locomotive, driven by steam acting against turbine blades rather than conventional piston cylinders. This locomotive, therefore, did not exhibit the characteristic chugging exhaust, but only a steady whoosh of its turbine. Two other turbines were built, one for the Chesapeake and Ohio and the other for the Norfolk and Western called the *Jawn Henry*. But despite the Niagaras and T-1's and turbines, the pinnacle of the locomotive builders craftsmanship, the Iron Horse was uttering its dying breath. The diesel had surpassed the best the steam locomotive could offer.

While the foundries were designing new mammoth giants of the rails, another manufacturer named General Motors was busily at work building a vehicle that was designed to operate on rails, which had a sixteen-cylinder V-type diesel engine connected to a direct-current electrical generator. This supplied power to traction motors which powered the vehicle. In areas of World War II where railroads were demolished by Allied bombardment and where motive power was needed, the diesel-electric locomotive was impressed into service, exported from the shops of General Motor's Electro-Motive Division.

The basic diesel engine was patented by Rudolf Diesel back in 1892. In the early 1930's General Motors had experimented with diesel engines, and under the hand of Charles Kettering, the inventor, and Alfred P. Sloan, the businessman, the two cycle diesel engine and the electrical transmission was developed into the basic framework of the diesel-electric locomotive.

Both American Locomotive and Baldwin Locomotive Works also experimented with the diesel. American believed that the diesel might have potential. Baldwin did not. Lima didn't even attempt a diesel until much later. American was able to build a limited version of passenger diesels and some diesel-electric switching locomotives, but its wartime effort and its postwar selling effort was in steam locomotives, and fierce competitors they were to Baldwin and Lima. And they had hopes, because the majority of railroad presidents at war's end were equally convinced that the Iron Horse, the same Iron Horse that blazed such a glorious trail in the past, would forge an even more glorious trail in the future. But then, several things happened, almost all at once.

In the postwar years and particularly 1947 and

1948 there occurred a marked inflationary spiral of labor demands for increased wages and resultant price hikes by the industries to offset these rising costs. The outcome was to push the cost of operating the railroads higher than railroad managements felt they could go. The railroads, being regulated by the Interstate Commerce Commission, could not raise their rates to keep pace with rising costs as easily as nonregulated private industry. On top of this came a disastrous coal strike which virtually shut down the railroads for a period of time and later raised the price of coal to where railroad executives studied operating cost reports intensively.

The travelling public during the war had been exposed to just about everything the railroads could make roll to accommodate the flood tide of wartime transportation. At the conclusion of the war, the railroads decided to promote passenger travel by rail and as a result replaced a moderate amount of their antiquated rolling stock with the most modern of streamliners. But would the travelling public still enjoy viewing the landscape through picture windows obscured by black smoke and the lurching and jolting characteristics of the steam locomotive? Of course not, they reasoned. So, for tangible operating cost reductions as well as timely advertising fodder, the passenger diesel became an extremely desirable machine to buy.

Even before the bombs had rained down on Pearl Harbor Electro-Motive Division unveiled Number 103, a streamlined, four-unit diesel-electric locomotive which astonished even the most skeptical railroad executives, surpassing performance records on the flatlands and over the mountains of twenty railroads. In 1944, a fleet of sixteen duplicates of this prototype freight diesel called the FT by its builder went into service on the Burlington, its president, Ralph Budd, already convinced that its future passenger power lay in diesels. By war's end, more FT's had rolled out of the LaGrange shops, and by 1947 American Locomotive Company had begun to mass-produce its flat-nosed FA-1 series of freight diesels. General Motors had announced the F-3, an increasingly more powerful version of the early prototype.

And finally, the inhabitants of many cities had decided that the steady black pall of smoke that hung over its buildings, the principal source of which was the railroad yards and engine terminals, had to come to a halt. Many a civic legislative body was petitioned by constituents demanding an end be put to the steady rain of soot and cinders, the night-like days where at times the smoke became so bad that lights had to be turned on, and the choking, foul air. The more sensitive ones listened at first. In the years to follow other city councils would listen. But as each one did, and took action, the order went out to the railroads: "The steam engine must go!"

The railroad executives, from presidents to superintendents of track to superintendents of motive power to marketing and sales management listened. And then they took a look at their operations very, very closely.

They saw how they were harboring a collection of old wheezing smoke-belching specialists on their property. The yard engine couldn't go out to pull a fast freight or could it ever think of pulling the crack limiteds. All it could do was switch. When it wasn't pushing and pulling cars, it was sitting idle with coal burning and steam escaping out of the safety valves. The freight locomotives couldn't pull the express trains, the small local freight engines were too big to switch in the yards and too small to pull heavy main-line freights. The heavy freight engines would fall through the small trestles over the creeks where the branch lines ran. And so, the roundhouses were always full of these individualistic machines, all emitting clouds and clouds of smoke which didn't make the division superintendent's job any happier, as he answered irate phone calls from anguished city halls.

Still worse, whenever repair time rolled around, as it did all too often, the parts required for a small freight engine were not the same ones required for a powerful passenger locomotive like the Niagara. There even was little interchangeability between various classes of the same kind of locomotive. As a result, many parts had to be forged individually in the locomotive shops and part warehouses either couldn't stock enough parts for a given repair cycle or else were overstocked with parts that would seldom be used. The superintendent of motive power looked at the costs of maintaining the steam locomotives, now made infinitely worse through two rounds of labor contract negotiations — and when the diesel salesman began to talk, he was ready to listen.

Out on the main line, the superintendent of track was also ready to listen. The steam locomotive was basically a flailing, wildly plunging mechanical monster that was guided and kept in control only by the roadbed and the track. Let there be a weakened section of roadbed, a faulty rail, a loosened flange plate, and a powerful freight would jump the track causing a possible major rail disaster. Consequently, a constant surveillance of the track was necessary because of the pounding it was forced to take under the churning drive wheels of the Iron Horse. And often as not, there would be as many as 250 to 500 men out on the division replacing rail or ties or re-ballasting or tightening flanges, switches, and cross-over sections. The track superintendents asked this question, "Why have a 500,000 pound runaway steam locomotive beat up the rails and the roadbed when a five-unit diesel with each unit weighing in at 220,000 pounds or so could do the same job without punishing the track hardly at all?" The answer to that question doomed the Niagaras and the Mohawks when the diesel salesman came to call.

In the president's office, still other questions were asked. The chief topics of discussion centered about a tender subject called sustained performance. From the few diesels the railroads had ordered in 1944 to either prove the claims of its backers or else yield to the modern steam locomotive came reports such as 110 cars being moved at sixty miles per hour over huge distances, 5000- and 6000-ton trainloads moving where only 2800-ton trainloads had been possible behind steam. These caused an excited railroad management to warm its hands with glee.

The men who were forming up the marketing and advertising campaigns for the new streamliners they were planning to introduce to the travelling public had cause to rejoice as well. Their magnificent new passenger liners on the steel rail would be powered by 2000- and 4000-horsepower diesels insuring their passengers a smooth ride and taking a little off the edge of these trains in terms of operating costs. And so, the railroad managements picked up the chant: "The steam engine must go!"

And go it did. The orders for new steam locomotives dropped sharply. By 1947, only 72 new steam locomotives were installed on all railroads. On June 16, 1948, the first of the steam locomotive builders, American Locomotive Company, turned out the last steam locomotive in its long history; thereafter it produced nothing but diesels. The remaining builders competed fiercely for what little steam locomotive business remained, and by 1953 the order books showed zero for new steam locomotives. By then, the competition had subsided. Baldwin and Lima had merged, becoming Baldwin-Lima-Hamilton. While managing to build a small amount of diesel-electric locomotives, this company would never again regain its former prominence as a locomotive builder.

Even the most modern of the postwar steam locomotives could not keep up with the diesel in any respect. The diesel could pull more tonnage faster and at greater savings than anything dependent on coal that existed on the rails. In the yards, switching was accomplished at half the cost of what it had been before the arrival of the diesel yard switcher, and the railroad ceased to become the target of enraged smoke-abatement committees. Passengers riding behind the 4000-horsepower diesel-electrics in their streamlined coaches and Pullmans travelled to their destinations in smooth, clean comfort compared to what had been available before.

And behind the new diesel locomotives, a steady funeral procession began. From the huge locomotive terminals of Altoona and Collinwood and Roanoke, the old veterans of the rails were led in long, melancholy trains to the yards of the steel mills, where their final dismemberment would begin to the hiss of the acetylene torch and the thud of falling steel. There would be no services pronounced, no eulogies read, no ceremonies performed. It was, in the strictest sense, a business operation.

The Iron Horse went to its funeral in a manner of glory. The iron from locomotives is called Class 24 heavy-melting railroad scrap, highly desired by steel mills. A locomotive and tender combination could bring anywhere from $4000 to $12,000 depending upon its weight and the current value of the scrap market. From the storage track, the Iron Horse passed through the ritual of having its number plate, the builder's plate, and its bell cut away. These relics have been eagerly sought by railroad collectors everywhere and remain today as valued mementoes of the Age of Steam, along with highly expensive scale models of the original prototypes and a collection of hi-fi recordings of the steam locomotive's former greatness.

The trains of dead steam locomotives were heart-piercing to the railroad buffs that had watched them for so long. Moving at 25 miles per hour or less because of mechanical trouble which might occur (and frequently did) to these now-derelicts of the rails, the trains had these locomotives specially rigged for this last voyage. And roll they did, along the banks of Lake Erie bound for Republic Steel and Bethlehem Steel; past the corn fields of Illinois and Indiana headed for the open hearths of Gary, Indiana; out of the mountains of West Virginia headed for the Weirton scrap yards.

Perhaps the most poignant scene was the long train of dead locomotives rolling around the Horseshoe Curve west of Altoona. Here the famed Curve had echoed and re-echoed to the sound of these mighty locomotives. Now only the slow droning of the diesel at the head of this train could be heard, while the dead engines squeaked and groaned and swayed as the train moved slowly along. In a park in the middle of the Curve a K-4 Pacific sat, enshrined by the railroad it served so well, as if to watch this melancholy train pass. Soon, the last train such as this will have left, and children of generations yet to come will pause by the fence to look at this K-4 and ask, "Daddy, what's that?"

In the cities, the clouds of grime and fumes are still there, although the pall of black smoke and soot and the rain of cinders have passed with the death of the Iron Horse. There is a new name for the choking fumes and foul smog — Air Pollution. The automobile, the factory, and even the bonfire are blamed. The network of freeways and highways with its thousands and thousands of cars are now the new targets of the pollution control bodies which first came to grips with the Iron Horse. Many of these people who vigorously attacked the railroad in 1947 are now beginning to consider it as a means of salvation from the emission of carbon monoxide and oxides of nitrogen spewing forth from the exhausts of the long lines of automobiles and trucks inching their way forward along the choked and jammed freeways and expressways of our cities. Thus, the passing of the Iron Horse, while it solved the problem of the black smoke emission, did not end the air pollution problem.

It would take another generation, aided by the technological revolution started on the railroads in discarding the steam locomotive mainly as a cost-improvement to accomplish that. The passing of the Iron Horse marked the first step in The Transition of the Railroads.

There would be more.

This is the steam locomotive . . .
Some called it a smoke-belching nusiance . . .
Others referred to it in stronger terms . . .
But to those who sat in its cab, and to those admired it
from trackside, it was affectionately called . . . the iron
horse.

By night . . .

. . . the steam would hiss in its boilers as it sat under the dimly lit station platform on a warm July night, clad in its streamlined mantles, waiting for the signal which would send it streaking over the countryside with the night express . . .

. . . or by day . . .
The afternoon local would chug along with its 30-car train behind an unglamorous light freight engine designed for branch line service only.

The Iron Horse was a machine of thundering power . . .
(*Courtesy Pennsylvania Railroad*)

. . . or flashing speed . . .
Blasting over the Alleghenies with long black trains of
coal from the mines or racing over the crossing at 85
miles per hour with the mail and express.

The steam locomotive was the means by which most of
the freight . . .

. . . all of the mail . . .

. . . and most of the passengers travelled in the Northeastern United States.

It pushed . . .

. . . and it pulled.

Some were very big . . .

. . . and others were very small.

The steam locomotive was first and foremost an individual with respect to its duties on the railroad. The huge articulated compounds like the 7535 were built for heavy freight tonnage over the Pennsylvania mountains. The slender light Pacifics saw duty on the slow passenger locals. The old Ten-Wheelers worked the very remote branch lines like New York Central's Hojack branch with local freights. This individuality created a restriction. A locomotive built for one class of service could not possibly be used for any other class of service.

Nowhere was the Iron Horse more of an individual than in the heavy duty freight engine. Locomotives varied widely in their design from railroad to railroad, even though they were used for the same purpose. In addition, locomotives even on the same railroad were represented by many types and classes. They were even called by different names. The New York Central called their freight locomotives Mohawks, in honor of the river these swift but powerful steam engines paralleled. Other railroads such as the Illinois Central called their freight locomotives Mountains, based on the wheel arrangement they possessed.

Some of the modern steamers sprouted large metal smoke deflectors, a device borrowed from steam locomotives in service in Europe. The New York Central used these devices extensively on their steam locomotives built in the mid-1940's.

The very spirit of the railroad it served was reflected
in the way the Iron Horse appeared on each of the various railroads. If there was indeed any trademark the
railroad could exhibit, it was truly their individual
design of steam locomotives. Standardization in the
days of steam was an unheard-of thing.

But a new locomotive had arrived . . .

. . . while we were pushing ahead with our diesel program . . . the rest of the industry was sticking with steam power. Outside of one attempt made by a group of builders in the late thirties, no manufacturer in this country, other than ourselves, brought out a diesel powered freight locomotive until after World War II. Aside from switchers, it might be said we were first everywhere on the railroads of this country with diesel power . . . ALFRED P. SLOAN JR., *My Years With General Motors*. New York, Doubleday and Company, 1964.

42

All at once the Iron Horse stood in twilight . . .

. . . however, the locomotive builders and many railroad skeptics did not think so at the time. There were the new, powerful steam locomotives coming that would rapidly reassert the supremacy of steam. A product of the finest efforts of the builders' art, a culmination of over a hundred years craftsmanship in locomotive construction, and a great effort in the finest applications of engineering, these new machines would in no time send the diesel off the rails for good . . .

. . . or so they thought.

The Niagara made its appearance in 1946. It weighed in at close to 500,000 pounds on the rails, could pull a 20-car streamliner at sustained speeds of 85 miles per hour, or was capable of pulling a fast freight consisting of 70 to 100 cars at a speed of 60 miles per hour. The New York Central ordered 25 of these locomatives and used them primarily in passenger service.

These locomotives performed just as its builder, American Locomotive Corporation, said they would . . . they were, with other classic streamers, one of the finest of their kind.

The Pennsylvania Railroad unveiled two even more startling examples of the advances made in steam locomotives . . .

One was a streamlined compound-type locomotive that could be capable of high speeds over the Alleghenies as well as over the flatlands of Ohio and Indiana.

. . . the other was a steam turbine locomotive which made no characteristic chugging sound, but rather a steady whoosh from a Westinghouse-built steam turbine. *(Courtesy Pennsylvania Railroad)*

With the advent of the new advances in steam locomotive technology, the Iron Horse tried to rally . . .

. . . to keep its place on the rails . . .

. . . But for every fast freight a steam locomotive might
pull . . .

. . . the diesel could pull it faster.

In test after test and trial after trial, the story was always the same—no matter what the steam locomotive could do in the way of hauling heavy freight tonnage, the diesel could top it by half again as much—no matter how many dollars it cost the railroads to maintain the Iron Horse, the diesel's upkeep was always many dollars less. These were figures of efficiency and economy even the staunchest supporter of steam power could not overlook.

53

The legendary Hudson . . .

... and the newest of them all, the Niagara ...

the mighty Mohawk ...

would soon pull their last run.

For no matter what the Iron Horse could do . . .

. . . the diesel could do it better.

The only locomotive unaffected by the diesel revolution . . .

. . . was the "pure" electric.

"If you can't beat them, join them."

The steam locomotive couldn't even follow that old adage.

(*Courtesy Pennsylvania Railroad*)

The Iron Horse drew its last breath, steaming off to the dead track.

On these dead tracks, the steam locomotives were made ready for their last trip to the scrapyard. The number plates and bells, along with such other mementoes as the builders plates and throttle levers were cut away, to become prized souvenirs by railroad buffs that wanted some reminder of the Age of Steam, now rapidly passing. These switch engines, the preparation work completed, now sit in readiness for their last run.

To the enthusiast of steam, the funeral train of the Iron Horse was a pitiful sight—where these black monsters once blasted their exhausts to the skies above, they were now quietly towed along at a speed of 20 miles an hour to avoid mechanical failure en route to the bonepit. Box-cars were spaced in between the locomotives to distibute the weight of the train evenly. The perfect setting for such a funeral train is provided in the world-famous Horseshoe Curve west of Altoona, where a K-4 Pacific has been spared the funeral train and is permanently enshrined there.

*(Courtesy Pennsylvania Railroad)*

Only the memories of the Iron Horse remained . . .

. . . as the new diesels now reigned over the steel rails.

# 2

## The Diesel Takes Over

What sort of a machine was this, that in the space of less than a decade had come upon the railroad properties and sent the 35,000 steam locomotives the railroad had on its active roster in 1947 off to the scrap yard? The dieselization of American railroads in the 1950's was an event of revolutionary proportions as technological changes go. Was the diesel some instantaneous innovation which caught railroad executives at a time when they were harassed by aroused smoke control officials on one side and deluged by skyrocketing costs on the other side, or was it a product which was developed over many years before it finally won acceptance?

The answer can be considered as "yes" to both questions. The diesel was invented back in 1892 and developed very slowly in the following decade. Yet, the rush to dieselization became a stampede when the F-3 was announced, for in this locomotive all of the ills plaguing railroad management entrusted with operations were wiped out on a scale of cost savings such as rarely is seen in industry. Let us see how this had come about.

In 1892 the German inventor Rudolph Diesel received the original patent for the engine that was to bear his name. It was a crude affair, and the year was 1897 before the first successful diesel engine was completed, a one-cylinder, four-cycle twenty-

five-horsepower machine. The principle of the diesel differed from the conventional gasoline engine in that on the first two strokes of the piston, air was taken in and then compressed, until it reached a temperature in excess of 1000°F. On the completion of the second or compression stroke, fuel oil was injected directly to the cylinder, thereby igniting and forcing the third and fourth strokes — ignition and evacuation of the exhaust. Hence, the diesel engine could convert fuel directly to energy, without using a secondary medium such as boiling water as in the steam engine, or else requiring evaporation of the fuel in a carburetor as in the typical gasoline engine.

The diesel engine was characterized as efficient — but overweight. The average weights of the first diesel engines were about 250 to 260 pounds per horsepower. Being overweight, the diesel engine had been used chiefly in pumping stations, small power generation plants, and in some — but not many — marine applications. From its initial beginnings, the Germans had made great strides to improve the diesel engine, reducing the weight down to about sixty pounds per horsepower, many of these engines being utilized in the U-boat fleet of World War I and some being used in railcars. In the United States, the diesel was evolving in much the same basic manner. Some industrial switchers were built in the early 1930's, and a few railcars emerged in that period as well.

The railroads also experimented with gasoline-engine railcars and gas-electric railcars as well. These "doodlebugs" were curiosities in their day, being in the main converted baggage-coach combinations with six- or eight-cylinder gasoline engines developing up to 400 horsepower. These engines were coupled to a DC generator which generated current sufficient to drive traction motors which powered the driving wheels. The gas-electrics soon became capable of hauling a passenger coach on some local passenger runs, but had their limitations as to speed and weight. Many Eastern railroads used this gas-electric during the 1930's, and while it gave them some experience with non-steam power, it supplied little else.

In the 1930's there also appeared on several railroads a type of Janus-like locomotive with a cab mounted at dead center and sloping hoods protruding from each end. These switch engines, also powered by gasoline-driven engines, did routine switching on many industrial spurs; but already a pattern was beginning to emerge — these curiosities of the rails were doing the same job the whistling teakettle steam switchers were doing, and at less cost.

Back at Electro-Motive Corporation, which had turned out many a doodlebug for the railroads, some basic work was going into the problem of the diesel engine's weight. General Motors had acquired EMC in 1930, and by then EMC still could not produce a diesel engine of less than sixty pounds per horsepower. It was fairly obvious by then that a decided limitation was at hand to the kind of non-steam locomotive that could be produced. The gasoline engine, while it was certainly light enough to pose no problems in propelling itself around, could only produce up to 400 horsepower in eight cylinders — enough for a two-car passenger train, but not much else. The diesel engine, on the other hand, was so overweight that it, too, could be used at best in nothing more than railcars and small switchers. Both EMC's president Harold Hamilton and the inventive genius of General Motors' Charles W. Kettering were wrestling with the problem of the diesel engine adaptable for railroad service. By 1932, Kettering had settled upon the idea of a two-cycle diesel engine, one where fresh air would be blown into the cylinder as the exhaust gases were leaving it, thus creating one power stroke (where the fuel was ignited) per two total piston strokes in place of the

one power stroke for four total strokes inherent in the four-cycle engine. Two such two-cycle engines were used, with some degree of apprehensiveness by General Motors, for the power exhibit at the Century of Progress Exposition in Chicago in 1933.

The success of these new two-cycle diesel engines made the breakthrough in railroading. Ralph Budd, president of the Chicago, Burlington and Quincy Railroad, ordered this engine to power the *Burlington Zephyr,* then being developed in the plant of E. G. Budd in Philadelphia. The streamliner race was on, for the Union Pacific was interested in a streamliner of its own and had already drawn an immense public reaction when its plans were announced. After experiencing the feared technical bugs in the new engines and overcoming them, the *Zephyr* emerged from Philadelphia to set new speed records from Denver to Chicago. The Union Pacific ordered 1200-horsepower diesel engines from General Motors to power such trains as the *City of Denver* and *City of San Francisco* series of streamliners.

From that point onward, developments followed rapidly in terms of the evolution of the diesel locomotives. Electro-Motive Corporation sold its first batch of yard switchers to the railroads in 1936. By 1940 over a hundred diesel-electric passenger locomotives were produced and in service. The first demonstrator locomotive for freight service rolled out of the newly acquired LaGrange, Illinois plant of Electro-Motive the same year. But perhaps the greatest breakthrough in bringing the diesel to the railroads of America lay not in the *Zephyr* nor in the fleet of passenger diesels being acquired by the railroads in limited numbers, but in a major policy decision laid down at General Motors the year the huge corporation decided to build finished locomotives. This decision was to the effect that Electro-Motive Corporation would not attempt to build to the different standards and specifications demanded by each railroad but instead would build a *standardized* product, for *all* railroads, the merits of which would be given a fair trial before the railroads would be allowed to write their own specifications as to how the locomotives were to be. In short, the influence of the railroads upon the steam locomotive builders in their design and manufacture which had produced the Mohawks for the New York Central and the Mountains for the Pennsylvania, two locomotives designed for heavy freight service but with no other similarity, would not hold sway with this builder of a new form of locomotive power. In time, the railroads would worship this decision when interchangeability of parts and the later development of the General Purpose (second-generation) locomotive would come to pass.

Over at American Locomotive, all was not idle in the development of the diesel-electric locomotive either. Alco had perfected a 2000-horsepower passenger diesel locomotive in 1940 and had also made deliveries to several railroads of these streamlined units. But the area where Alco had made heavy inroads on the diesel locomotive market which had begun to develop was in the yard switcher market. Rugged 600, 1000, and 1500 horsepower yard diesel-electric locomotives began to roll out the doors of the Schenectady locomotive builder with increasing volume in the months prior to Pearl Harbor. Unlike Electro-Motive, however, there was not so vigorous an effort to produce a freight diesel, largely due to the *rapport* which existed between locomotive builders and the railroads not to violently overturn an allegiance to the steam locomotive that had been cultured for over a century. Thus, while Alco produced diesel-electric yard engines, it also produced the steam-powered giants of the rails which were delivered during the 1940's. Hence, when World War II came to the United States, Alco was classed as a builder of steam locomotives and heavy machinery. While Electro-Motive was free to continue developmental work on the freight locomotive, Alco's production was restricted to the manufacture of steam locomotives to be added to America's growing wartime transportation system, to the production of tanks and other heavy military vehicles, and to the manufacture of diesel-electric yard locomotives of 1000-horsepower or less. The other locomotive builders were under the same War Production Board restrictions and hence, the development of the freight diesel was given over to Electro-Motive. The belief among all of General Motors' competitors and on not a few railroads as the war began was that Electro-Motive was crazy in pushing the freight diesel. But late in 1939, the freight diesel indeed became a reality.

In 1940, as the tricolor of France was lowered and the swastika was raised over the Eiffel Tower, the statistics were being compiled in huge volumes over the performance of Number 103, a green and yellow diesel freight locomotive that was the prototype of a flood of freight diesels yet to come. Over the lines of the Pennsylvania, Number 103 pulled an unheard of 5000 tons of freight; the best any steam freight locomotive could haul was 2800 tons. The 103 demonstrated that the fuel costs per 1000 gross

ton-miles could be slashed more than half compared to competing steam power. Wherever the 103 went, railroaders that had only known the sounds and capabilities of the Iron Horse thought they were on the wrong end of some monstrous hoax. This streamlined giant was so unlike the doodle-bugs and the box cab units that so frequently would sputter out and die on the main line to be ignominiously towed back to the shops. It did not seem possible for such a machine to keep running. But run it did, week after week, month after month, all throughout the war years.

The railroad executives also harbored something else besides disbelief. Most Eastern roads possessed adequate coal supplies on their lines, and they believed that since their coal sources were so easily accessible, there just could never be the possibility of getting rid of every steam locomotive they owned. About 40 per cent of all the freight they hauled was coal. Furthermore, the locomotive builders such as Alco, Baldwin, and Lima assured their railroad customers that the new steam locomotives yet to come would beat once and for all even the now fabled 103. However, a series of token orders followed the 103's tour of twenty railroads when the wartime press of traffic became too much for their already overworked rosters of steam locomotives. A dozen or so were ordered by the Baltimore and Ohio. The Pennsylvania placed a slightly larger order. The New York Central ordered only eight units. All eyes were upon this token fleet of diesels in the East, while out West, larger numbers of these fleets of diesels were ordered by railroads even harder put to stretch out their existing steam engine pools.

By the end of World War II the results of these early diesels had left mixed feelings. In the West, railroad executives were just beginning to think in terms of total dieselization. In the East, the railroad operating personnel were enthusiastic about the diesel but were still mainly interested in adding diesels only to the yards and on passenger service, partially out of fear of disturbing their coal customers, partially out of still-lingering disbelief. By then, American Locomotive, who had seen the handwriting on the wall with the success of EMD's 103, had a competitor in the final stages of development: a flat-nosed 1600-horsepower model. Baldwin was still totally committed to steam, as was Lima. Meanwhile EMD had followed through with the Model F-3, which was destined to be the diesel that would send thousands upon thousands of steam locomotives to the scrap heap.

By 1947, the railroads had seen enough of their sagging profit figures to have made up their minds once and for all. They had experienced costs rising out of all proportions and had been forced to suspend nearly all operations due to a prolonged coal strike. Hence, the diesel would be added as soon as possible to retire the pool of steam locomotives that had been demonstrated as cost headaches to the men that ran America's railroads.

By the early 1950's whole sections of the principal railroads of the East were under complete dieselization, the balance of their steam power having been herded off to their western divisions in the prairie states of Ohio, Indiana, and Illinois. East of Cleveland, the New York Central was completely diesel powered and the Alco and EMD diesels had made sizable inroads on many areas west of Cleveland as well. The Pennsylvania had removed many of its steam locomotives to storage as the streamlined F-3's droned over the Alleghenies. The Baltimore and Ohio as well as many another railroads whose coal hauling constituted a major share of their business discovered that it was far less costly even to haul the long coal trains behind growling five- and six-unit diesels than to use their steam locomotives. The steady confident growl of 16-cylinder diesel engines replaced the stacatto exhaust of steam locomotives in New England, along the Hudson, over the Alleghenies, past steel mills and grain elevators, along the Great Lakes — everywhere in the Northeast.

The coaling stations and water towers were torn down over the locomotive terminals, since they now served only as a haven for the flocks of pigeons that roosted there. The track pans where steam locomotives would gulp water at speeds of 70 to 80 miles per hour were ripped out, along with the water treatment plants to prevent scale from fouling up the boiler tubes. The roundhouses were modified and renovated to accommodate their new diesel tenants. Oil fueling facilities were erected.

The many iron forging shops were dismantled, a costly item now all at once eradicated by the parts standardization which had proven to be one of the biggest areas of saving the diesel-electric locomotive had brought to the railroads. A new cylinder head to replace a worn-out one on a switcher was the same one that could be used to replace its counterpart on a passenger locomotive. The traction motors on any F-3 freight diesel could be used on any other F-3 diesel. Huge warehouses containing parts for the steam locomotives were condensed into one central warehouse which stocked parts for the entire system. Indeed, the need for many locomotive shops throughout the railroad system had passed and many of these were closed down and razed, leaving diesel repair work to be performed at one or two centrally located shops rather than at many smaller ones. Thus, even more savings were realized by the simple economies of scale that standardization afforded.

In operations, the diesel had even more to show. Where before a yard engine crew would get its steam-powered switch engine in the locomotive terminal and deadhead down the main line to an area where it was to begin switching, the crew would now report directly to the freight terminal or passenger station location where switching was needed. There would sit the diesel switcher, ready for a full shift's work. The shift completed, the crew would either be relieved by another crew or else would shut down the engine, set its brakes, lock it up, and drive off for home. In the days of steam, the crew of any freight locomotive could be guaranteed a spartan-like existence on a run. In the summer, the heat of day together with the roaring fire just in front of them behind the bulkhead made the cab an infernal place to work. In the winter, the engineer attempting to sight down the immense length of boiler would have his face cut to ribbons mercilessly by snow, sleet, and cold. Clouds of steam and fog would forever blind his vision, causing him to either restrict his speed or else charge ahead, swearing and cursing all the time, hoping the fireman opposite him could be able to see the signals along the track. On some railroads the cab was so small that there was room only for the engineer and fireman to operate. Since the head-end brakeman was also a part of the crew up front, the only place for this gentleman to ride was a "doghouse" located atop the locomotive tender just back of the coal bunker. In days of rain, snow, heat, or cold, this man's work day was extremely horrible. It was probably because of the intense attraction of the railroad in the lives of these men that they manned these steam locomotives day in and day out. A special breed of man was required to be a railroader in the days of steam.

With the advent of the diesel, the crew would climb aboard to a roomy cab which afforded them a clear, unobstructed view down the length of track. When the diesel was first introduced, many an engineer snorted in disgust over this new-fangled machine, but after a short stretch of time diesel school and diesel service were awarded to the men possessing the highest seniority, so vastly improved were the working conditions. The cab was infinitely cleaner than the most modern steam locomotive. The heat was there in the summertime, but it wasn't any different from the heat one would put up with while driving his own car. Because of the enclosed cab, the icy blasts of winter were a forgotten thing unless perhaps it was necessary to look back along the length of locomotive while backing up to a string of cars before coupling on to them. The fireman and the head-end brakeman could also ride up front in the cab with no space restriction, and with neither coal to shovel nor steam pressure to constantly watch, they became jolly travelling companions for the engineer, seated at his ivory-painted control box as the F–3 droned onward through the countryside with its mile-long freight. One day the existence of the fireman aboard freight and yard diesels would be challenged, but for the time being what was once a dirty, dangerous, and cruel job was transformed overnight into one which allowed the locomotive fireman to sit relatively undisturbed and read everything from Plato to Mickey Spillane. Indeed, the time-honored costume of the engineer, the blue pin-striped coveralls, cap, and the red bandana had been laid in mothballs. Some engineers were even so contemptuous of the dead Iron Horse as to wear dress suits while behind the controls.

Seniority, always a topic of great interest of the engineers and firemen and the Brotherhoods that represented them, was even more keenly exercised with the coming of the diesel. It had to, because the diesel had curtailed significantly the numbers of men entering the operating ranks of the railroads. The trains had grown from 75–90 cars in length to over 150 cars long. The diesel was capable of being extended into locomotives of five or six individual units in length. As such, with carloadings in 1953 showing a decline from 1947 levels by six million units to a net level of 38 million units, the number of trains necessary to move this volume of traffic was substantially reduced. Railroad executives freely admitted that if it were not for the economies of dieselization, the railroads would have had a much more dismal financial picture than was the case during the recession years of 1953 and 1954.

Meanwhile, at the locomotive builders' plants, new developments were in the making and were well underway. One of the noticeable factors of the diesel locomotive when it made its first great rush onto the railroads in the late 1940's was that despite the interchangeability of parts within the diesel engine itself, the locomotive unit was still a specialist to some degree by virtue of its traction motor gearing. Thus, there existed the passenger locomotive that excelled in the 60 to 85 mile per hour range but nobody in his right mind would dare use such a locomotive in heavy freight service. The freight diesel set new performance records by moving trains of heavy tonnage at relatively high speeds, but could not be used in passenger service because it lacked steam generators to heat the train as well as being unable to operate at nearly the sustained high speeds of their passenger counterparts.

The diesel yard engines were perhaps the closest thing the railroads had by the late 1940's to a general-purpose locomotive. They could switch tirelessly night and day in the yards, as well as work out on the main line or haul the branch line locals. They had the capability of running in multiple-unit lengths, which enabled several of them to be operated by one crew in double and triple units for extremely heavy switching service such as moving long trains up the "hump" in a gravity-type classification yard. Like any mechanical equipment, the diesel-electric locomotive also failed on occasion, and more often than not, a three-unit combination of diesel-electric switching engines would go out to bring in the stalled train on the main line. By this time, American Locomotive Company had built a diesel-electric switcher that developed 1600 horsepower and could not only perform yard duties but was also observed to race along at high speeds with commuter trains and branch-line locals. This locomotive possessed basically the same power plant as the freight diesel and as a result it found its use also in heavy-duty freight service. This road-switcher American Locomotive manufactured was unique in that it possessed a raised cab which enabled it to be used as a switcher, yet it was every bit as powerful as its FA–1 freight diesel counterparts in that it could be run in multiple unit combinations geared down for pulling the heavy freights or else geared up for high-speed passenger service. Thus the RS–2, as American called it, was the first general-purpose diesel locomotive.

EMD was also hard at work on a general-purpose locomotive, while at the same time still committed to the basic streamlined freight locomotive it had pioneered so successfully. The F–7 freight diesel was announced two years after the F–3 made its debut and it continued the rush of the diesel onto the rails where the F–3 had left off. Basically an improved F–3, it possessed 1750 horsepower per unit and together with the upgraded Alco freight diesel became the last of the streamlined first-generation diesels, one which railroaders along the Pennsylvania would soon call "covered wagons" — owing to the totally enclosed engine rooms they possessed. Just after the F–7 freight diesel was announced, the shark-nosed GP–7 general-purpose road-switcher made her debut from General Motors. With this, the second-generation or general-purpose diesel had truly arrived on the railroad scene. Whatever steam power had survived the initial orders for freight diesels, passenger diesels, and yard locomotives was truly doomed by this most versatile locomotive.

The general-purpose diesel electric locomotive was known by many names on the railroads. Some called them "geeps," others called them "mules," still others called them "hood units." It was technically called a road-switcher, meaning it was capable of performing on any main-line or branch-line assignment as well as handling any yard assignment. And it did just that.

The road switcher pulled commuter and branch-line locals. It ran in triple-unit configuration to pull crack streamliners at speeds no less than their passenger diesel counterparts were doing. In the same three, four, and five-unit combinations, it pulled the long, heavy freights with the same or better performance records that the freight diesels were able to post. Interchangeability reached new levels; not only were parts and motors able to be substituted between the road switchers, the freight diesels, and the passenger diesels, but also the locomotive units themselves were now able to be interchanged so that a locomotive assigned to a freight could have any mixture of freight diesels and road-switchers in the string of individual units which made it up. Thus, the streamliner concept which had emerged with the 103 was now nearing extinction, as the demands from the financially-pressed railroads echoed for more power, more general-purpose adaptability, and more standardization.

In 1954 the declines in the carloadings and the commerce that was being transported over the railroads, particularly in the East, fell to alarmingly low levels, marked by the recession which had followed the Korean armistice and reflecting inroads made by the competition of trucks, airlines, and waterway traffic. The rapid pace by which the railways were ordering new diesels had fallen off, as the impetus for expanding dieselization was dulled by the prospects of red ink. Yet in 1954 the diesels had accounted for over 80 per cent of all passenger, freight, and yard operations. The diesels the railroads were ordering were all of the general-purpose variety. However, in 1955 there occurred a sudden reversal of traffic patterns on the railroads as the economy abruptly shifted from recession to upturn and the railroads were caught with a locomotive shortage that their rosters of diesel locomotives couldn't solve.

The rows and rows of old steam locomotives awaiting final dispatch at the scrapyards were suddenly recalled to life. The fires were rekindled in their massive fireboxes, steam once again spurted through cylinders beginning to rust with disuse, repairs were hastily made — and the Iron Horse began its last spurt before the coming of total extinction. While the telegrams and purchase orders were winging their way to the sales centers of Alco and General Motors, and the telephones in the executive offices of these locomotive builders were frantically ringing, the steam locomotives of the East were once again blasting and thundering over the midwestern plains. At one point, the Cleveland Union Terminal, which had its pure electric locomotives removed for service elsewhere due to the diesel-electric locomotive takeover, found itself host to a fleet of steam engines as diesel availability became scarce throughout the New York Central System.

For the steam locomotive, it was a dying gasp. By 1955 most of the servicing facilities for steam locomotives had been removed or so neglected by disuse that in some remote areas coal had to be transferred directly from the coal hopper car to the locomotive tender, and water had to be taken aboard untreated from the nearest available fire hydrant. As 1956 dawned, the vanguard of the second-generation diesels arrived to retire this rag-tag fleet of steamers. These locomotives were all general-purpose road switchers, now upgraded to 2000 horsepower per unit, and were as superior to the original freight diesels as those first streamlined pioneers had been to the steam locomotives they displaced.

On May 2, 1957, the last steam locomotive ended its run on the New York Central in Cincinnati, dropped its fires, and went dead to become the last of the long line of locomotives consumed by the open-hearth furnace. On July 15, 1959 the last

Pennsylvania steam locomotive ended its service in New Jersey. The diesel takeover had been completed.

The economic effects of the diesel on a broad scale were not only felt by the railroad industry. The bituminous coal industry was so seriously affected by the wholesale conversion to diesels that it began large-scale movements to preserve and further entrench itself in its remaining outlets, as well as to develop new applications to regain the markets which so abruptly had been stripped away from it. In 1947, on the eve of the great conversion, the steam railroads had constituted the largest single consumer group of bituminous coal, with the electric utilities and steel mills the next largest coal users. By 1955 the market for bituminous coal for railroads had all but evaporated as the railroads were exceeding 90 per cent of their operations with diesels. The coal industry was therefore thrust into an immediate need for optimization of all their operations: from mining through preparation to final distribution to their customers. Thus, expeditious steps toward automation and mechanization of mining operations were undertaken with both the blessing of the United Mine Workers and the round-the-clock efforts of the coal operators to implement them. Included in these efforts were attempts in the Ohio Legislature to secure rights for an overland conveyor belt to haul coal from the Ohio River at East Liverpool to Lake Erie, thus posing serious competition to the railroads that controlled the movement of coal from the mines to the power plants and steel mills. Also underway was a series of feasability experiments with a coal slurry pipeline at Cadiz, Ohio, which had successfully demonstrated that coal could be moved from mine to user via a hydraulic pipeline, thus lowering the delivered cost of coal and avoiding the onrush of central nuclear power stations which after railroad dieselization could knock out the coal industry completely. Thus, the diesel had brought the coal industry up fighting. The railroads would soon begin to feel the lash.

At the moment, however, the railroads couldn't have asked for dieselization any sooner, as they were already feeling the severe pains of market losses in other areas than coal.

The rising tides of competition, the rising costs of operation of trains, the maintenance costs of the physical plant of the railroad, the accelerated decline of traffic through two recessions, and the failure of the railroad to regain completely its position in the intervening boom years made railroad executives breathe a sigh of gratitude that in 1947 they had given the green light to dieselization. For the diesel, in addition to effecting enormous cost savings in operation of trains and maintenance of track and motive power had opened the doorways wide to areas where even more savings could be reached.

The diesel, as we have mentioned, made the duties of the locomotive fireman infinitely easier. They were so easy, as a matter of fact, that the railroads began to ask some thought-provoking questions about whether the fireman was necessary at all. There were no more fires to tend, and with a diesel road switcher, it seemed highly unlikely that the fireman had to go back to the engine room to periodically inspect the diesel engines and generator as he had done with the "covered wagon" type freight diesels. Since the freight diesels carried toilet facilities on board for the crew's use, it was doubted whether the fireman's trips back to the engine room were to inspect the engines at all. The only justification for the fireman remaining on board the general-purpose road switchers was to call signals to the engineer, as he had done in steam days, owing to the long length of diesel hood extending from the cab. The fireman question would be formally raised after the third-generation diesel made its appearance.

The decision made back in 1935 by General Motors to produce a standardized model of a railroad locomotive unaffected by the same individual personality and desires of each railroad that had been expressed in the steam locomotives of the era also would have additional merits. When the diesel had shown its superiority over the steam engine in the immediate postwar period, the railroads readily acquiesced to this standardization, especially after their maintenance costs were drastically lowered. But something else also developed. The model and type locomotives which ran on the Erie railroad were the same model and type locomotives which could run on the Delaware, Lackawanna, and Western. The diesels which pulled merchandise freight over the Baltimore and Ohio had identical sister models droning over the Appalachian mountains with long coal trains on the Chesapeake and Ohio. The GP–7 and GP–9 road switchers on the Nickel Plate Road were no different than the GP–7 and GP–9's roaring across the midlands of Illinois along the Wabash. And the F–7 black and grey striped New York Central locomotives which raced through the middle of Upstate New York had their identical counterparts growling along the banks of the Ohio

72

on the Pennsylvania Railroad near the Golden Triangle of Pittsburgh, which basked in the clear blue skies made possible by the diesel's coming. Railroad executives who once were proud competitors now began to unroll their maps and overlay them, one atop the other, considering for the first time the colossal savings if economies of scale could be further realized by merger. After all, the diesel could be used anywhere, so the once formidable barrier of non-interchangeability of motive power was eliminated in the consideration of the possibilities of merging large railroad systems.

Hence, the full impact of the economics of the diesel still had not been entirely felt. But the potential was there, and a day was not long in coming when this, too, would be a topic of major consideration by the railroads of the East.

While the fallen giant lay in state with the people coming from far and near to pay their last respects . . .

. . . the new giant stood by.

The first freight diesels to be mass-produced were the series F-3 models built by Electro-Motive Division of General Motors. These were superseded by the F-7 series shown above which were rated at 1500 horsepower per unit and were the principal diesel units ordered by most of the railroads in their changeover from steam to diesel in the late 40's and early 1950's. Electro-Motive accounted for well over 70 per cent of all diesels sold in the great transition from steam to diesel.

There were no more fires to tend . . .

. . . and no more smoke to blot out the landscape.

In direct contrast to the individuality by which the steam locomotive was characterized, the diesels were the last word in standardization. The same model and type locomotive was produced for one railroad as it was for another. All that could tell them apart was the different color schemes each railroad saw fit to paint on these new locomotives.

The diesel was also able to pull freight after freight with maintenance so infrequent that it was available for duty 90 per cent of the time, as opposed to the 60 per cent availability of the steam engine.

An occasional trip to the wash rack seemed to be all the care this tireless machine required.

82

The first-generation diesels such as the Electro-Motive F-3 and F-7 were basically freight locomotives. However, several of them were equipped for service on crack streamliners, such as the Lackawanna's *Phoebe Snow* or the Santa Fe's *Chief.* Once designated for passenger service, however, these locomotives remained in this type of use. Thus, the freight diesel and the diesel equipped for passenger service, while they had interchangeable parts and looked basically alike, still could not be easily substituted for different types of service.

The second-generation diesel would change all that.

They called this new kind of diesel . . .

. . . the road switcher.

It did the switching in the yards . . .

. . . and a few sleek passenger trains as well.

. . . pulled the fast freights . . .

87

The first general-purpose diesels were built by American Locomotive, which although committed to the building of steam engines during World War II, managed to build a sizable number of diesel switchers. From these switching-type locomotives evolved the so-called "hood unit" such as the RS-2. This general-purpose diesel was second in popularity on the railroads only to the GP series of road-switchers which Electro-Motive introduced a few years later. The RS-2 was used extensively in heavy freight service and in commuter runs, as well as mail and express trains.

90

Baldwin-Lima-Hamilton, a company formed from two ex-steam locomotive builders entered the diesel market sufficiently late so as to capture only a small share of the market. Nevertheless, this builder also was producing road-switchers and one of the most powerful machines of the early diesel years was a 2400-horsepower locomative which was used mainly in heavy-duty freight service. Due to the dominance of the locomotive market by General Motors and Alco, not too many of these locomotives were built.

Unquestionably the most successful general-purpose diesel of them all was the GP series of road-switchers produced by Electro-Motive Division of General Motors. Thousands upon thousands of these locomotives were mass-produced like automobiles and found their way rapidly onto the nation's railways. The "geeps" as they were nicknamed by railroaders, were used everywhere—in the yards, on heavy freights, and in passenger service. So popular were these diesels with the railroads that by the late 1950's, Electro-Motive had discontinued its streamlined-type freight diesel from production.

By the late 1950's dieselization of the railroads was virtually completed. A technological revolution of the first magnitude had come about in the short space of ten years, commencing in 1947.

The long freights were moving now like they had never moved before—longer, faster, and smoother. With sky-rocketing costs of operation and reduced traffic plaguing the railroads as they passed through two periods of economic recession, the diesel could not have arrived at a more needed moment. The cost improvements which the diesel brought to the railroads did much to soften the impact of lowered revenues.

The diesels and the men that rode in their cabs had forged a new chapter in American Railroading. Both in fair weather . . .

. . . and in foul.

By day . . .

. . . and by night.

# 3

## The Vanishing Passenger Train

Before World War II, when people would think of the railroad at all, the vision that was conjured up was nearly always the racing, high-wheeled steam locomotive and its long olive-green string of baggage cars, Pullmans, diners, and coaches. There was the conductor with his dark blue cap and uniform studded with gold buttons adorned with gold braid, displaying the gold emblems of the railroad he served, and always in his hand was the huge round white-faced pocket watch that kept time to the split-second, which was attached to the heavy gold chain which was in turn securely attached to his dark blue vest. There was the friendly porter in his dark blue uniform who with a firm, unerring hand helped everybody young and old up and down the narrow stairways of the coach vestibule leading to that mysterious, fascinating world inside. There was the galvanizing call of "All Aboard!!" followed by the two sharp blasts of the steam engine up ahead. There was the accelerating rumble of the long coach which seemed to be charging off boldly to some lofty adventurous place far, far away. There was the dining car, with its savory smell of utterly delicious food drifting over the tables adorned with snow-white linens and glistening silverware, attended by waiters who must have waited upon kings and queens in their lifetimes. There was the challenging open-section sleeping car with its heavy velvet draperies that swayed to and fro as the travel-

ler tried to haul himself skyward to the upper berth and most often as not would either wind up sprawled in the middle of the swaying corridor or else an unwelcome bedfellow in the lower berth, depending, of course, on whom the occupant of the aforementioned lower berth happened to be. There was the huge palatial station in the glittering big city in which the train came to a final halt, where everybody scurried busily to and fro, either in the process of entering the marble-walled gateway to the huge metropolis or else in the equally hurried process of leaving it.

This was the excitement of travelling in the days prior to World War II. It was a genuine thrill compared to the feeling of pain a traveller received when he purchased a ticket aboard an airliner and discovered his life insurance had suddenly been cancelled. Train travel gave the traveller a solid feeling of security and confidence in knowing he was going somewhere as contrasted to the agonies of driving off in a 1939 Ford armed with overstuffed suitcases, pioneer determination, and utterly impossible road maps, and finally enduring untold frustrated anguish after encountering detours that weren't supposed to be there in the first place, and making several unstrategic turns in the road which more often than not narrowed down to a dirt cowpath, far away from any remote semblance of civilization.

Prior to World War II nearly everything and

everybody travelled by train because it was the only complete mode of intercity transit there was. The automobile was at best only a partially reliable means of going on a trip because mechanical breakdowns were not an uncommon occurrence and the prewar highway system was subject to unforeseen detours and mishaps, grade crossing delays, traffic jams encountered when passing through every town and hamlet, and cowherds crossing the road behind farmers that refused to move their animals faster despite a cacophony of blaring horns. The airline was a frightening means of going places by virtue of the fragile DC–2's and DC–3's that were in existence strictly due to the air mail contracts awarded them by the Federal Government. Thus, as in intercity freight, the railroads held a virtual monopoly.

When war came, the chief job of moving the huge masses of men from the farms and cities to the induction centers fell upon the railroads as did the immediately succeeding job of moving these same men now clad in khaki and green to the embarkation points from where they would fight and die on the fields of North Africa and in the jungles of the Solomons. The railroads impressed everything that would roll into this service. They dredged up coaches that had seen their former glory in the days immediately following the turn of the century. They scavenged Pullmans that were virtual relics and ripped out their musty moth-eaten interiors, installing benches in their place and sending them out on the great troop movement operation. The railroads even commandeered a fleet of boxcars, cut windows in their sides, installed the most dismal and primitive heat, light, and sanitary facilities, slapped a hurried coat of olive-green upon their riveted sides and sent them forth to join the ragtag fleet of anything that would haul human beings. The men that rode these rolling stock cars, although they would later find themselves in swampy foxholes or in burned-out French villages, would always remember the American railroad system and the miles after miles of jolting, grinding, creaking, and groaning as these trains rattled onward to their destinations.

The non-military travelling public would also never forget the overtaxed transportation system. Subject to a Federal 10 per cent tax to discourage wartime travel, they nevertheless found the necessity to travel from their home city to a distant city, either for family emergency or business or a million other private reasons. If they were fortunate enough to get a reserved coach seat on a plush streamliner such as the *Empire State Express* or a berth aboard the queen of the rails, the *Twentieth Century Limited*, their train trip would be pleasurably relaxing. On the other hand, if they found themselves stuffed aboard any of the vast numbers of lesser non-streamlined trains, the trip might be unforgettable at best and excruciating at the worst — in terms of lost sleep, delays, and general discomfort.

With the end of the war, the railroads embarked upon a massive rebuilding and rejuvenation program for their sagging and sorry passenger fleet. The wartime fleet of derelicts, museum pieces, and veritable cattle cars was retired, either permanently or else carefully put away for the day they would be for no apparent reason suddenly sprung loose anew on the travelling public. Heralding the new trains was a touring exhibit on wheels called the *Train of Tomorrow*, produced by General Motors, which gave the American public a preview of the innovations awaiting the railroad traveller. The public got its first look at the astra-dome lounge which was a raised glass enclosure running half the length of the roof of the car affording the traveller a panoramic view over the surrounding countryside. Below the raised dome observation gallery was a lounge which would outdo the swankiest nightclub. In the sleeping car exhibit spacious private compartments sported bedroom accommodations which had the Pullman passengers formerly accustomed to groping with the open section berths blinking with wide-mouthed amazement. The dining car exhibit featured gleaming stainless steel kitchens and panoramic windows at all tables. Heading this exhibit train was, of course, a powerful Electro-Motive 2000-horsepower E–7 diesel-electric locomotive. The people came from far and near to view with oh's and ah's this splendid forecast of what lay ahead for the travelling public. General Motors' *Train of Tomorrow* visited over a hundred cities across the nation, and by the time this train was completing its tour, the railroads were bringing their own modern fleet of passenger trains onto the rails. By the summer of 1947 over 1500 new passenger cars were placed in service by the railroads, with over a hundred streamlined trains in full operation. Over $1 billion in new cars and trains remained yet to be delivered.

On the Pennsylvania, spacious 44-seat reclining seat coaches raced from Chicago and St. Louis to Philadelphia and New York along with luxurious private-room Pullman accommodations. On the crack *Jeffersonian* between St. Louis and New York there was featured a newsreel theatre lounge. Other crack streamliners like the *Trail Blazer* had the very latest in diner-lounges: deep reclining parlor car seats, and gleaming stainless steel coffee shops which sparkled under soft fluorescent light. The *Broadway Limited* sported mobile train telephone service that allowed calls to be placed anywhere in the world from the patrician observation lounge. On the Wabash and the Baltimore and Ohio appeared the futuristic dome lounges aboard such trains as the *Banner Blue* and the *Columbian*, which raced across the prairies of Indiana or through the rugged headwaters of the Potomac in West Virginia.

The most heavily advertised rebuilding of its passenger fleet probably belonged to the New York Central. In magazines, over radio and television, and in newspapers came full page descriptions of The Great Steel Fleet, an entire array of streamliners which the New York Central unveiled. Leading this fleet was the elegant *Twentieth Century Limited*. Featured aboard this train were such conveniences as stenographic services, a barbershop, showers, and telephones. In short, the *Century* was a veritable hotel on wheels, and possessed the most lavish yet ultra-modern set of accommodations any traveller in the East would expect to find in a luxury hotel, let alone an overnight limited between Chicago and New York.

The new trains met with initial success. *Time Magazine* reported in August 1947 that although the cost of luxury trains had been heavy, the return had been worth the price. Many streamliners were booked solid with reservations. Illinois Central's *City of New Orleans* grossed in twelve months its $4 million cost. The Pullman accommodations aboard the *Texas Special* were 90 per cent booked compared to the 60 per cent bookings on the older open section Pullmans they replaced. An air of confidence was expressed by some railroaders that these new trains could finally put the carrying of passengers on a paying, profitable basis — even for the most unprofitable railroads maintaining passenger service.

The following month, the same *Time Magazine*, covering the debut of the new *Twentieth Century Limited* at Grand Central Station became more philosophical:

to them [the travelling public], the *Century's* elegances were a glimpse of unknown comfort, a far cry from the jolting realities of everyday railroad travel. The truth was that the U.S. citizen had been regarded by the railroads as a damn nuisance.

On the common [open section] Pullman the seasoned traveller knows he will be in bed no sooner and no later than the time the Pullman porter chooses to make up the berth . . . Commuter trains are dirty, late, and uncomfortable. For the smell of stale tobacco smoke, stained seat cushions, etc. the United States has no equal to a Pennsylvania Railroad day coach . . .
. . . Such evidences of rancor could not dislodge the railroads from their secure place in U.S. affections. American citizens are pridefully aware that their railway system is the world's greatest. Their tracks are the nation's sinews, their story part of the nation's legend.
. . . But as the American passenger gazed at lavish ads of the new promised land [the trains], he was bothered by a small, nagging doubt. There were radios in every room, nurseries, movie theatres, astra-domes, etc. Were these wonders for him or for the glamour trade? Would [*their*] trains still lurch like a moose on jolting roadbeds?

Perhaps what the passenger really wanted was less fluorescent and chromium and more plain old-fashioned convenience, courtesy, and on-time performance.

There was something troubling the railroads as well. Even though they had introduced a massive fleet of streamliners replete with the most ultra-modern appointments, staffed with hostesses, nurses, stenographers, and lounge atttendants in addition to the normal operating crew and the dining car crew, and pulled swiftly and quietly across the land by the most modern of diesel-electric power, their profit picture for their overall passenger train operations looked dismal. Paradoxically, modern streamliners were carrying nearly full trainloads on every run they made, yet the railroads were showing deficits in the operation of their passenger services.

There was a ready explanation for this enigma. The streamliners had found ready acceptance by the public and there was no problem in operating these trains. Even though the streamliners cost more to operate in terms of dining service, operations of the lounges, the many personalized attendant services such as porters, hostesses, stenographers, and the like, there was a profit because the trains ran fully occupied. The problem was not in the new plush streamliners, but in the multitude of branch-line locals and unglamorous main-line local passenger runs and commuter service runs which also operated and which ran relatively empty due to more convenient modes of travel offered by the automobile which was then swinging back to full-scale production after curtailment by the war, and by the bus lines which had modernized their obsolete coaches. The problem being thus diagnosed, the solution was readily apparent. The railroads would seek to abandon these unprofitable plug runs and concentrate on improving still further the lucrative passenger market that was patronizing their streamliner fleets extremely well. The solution was easy to arrive at, but the problem of bringing the solution into effect was something else, due to a regulatory body in Washington called the Interstate Commerce Commission and a whole host of lesser regulatory bodies on the state and local level.

In 1886 the Interstate Commerce Act had been passed; it put railroads at the head of a steadily lengthening list of industries classified as intending to exercise predatory practices of economic power, such as establishing or seeking to establish massive monopolies. Thus, public regulation was invoked to control the interstate carriers that had already effected a monopoly over transport of goods and services, with the Interstate Commerce Commission created as the regulatory body. This agency was empowered to hear all cases pertaining to establishment of rates, tariffs, and service. Before the railroad could make any adjustment in tariffs or discontinue service, approval of this regulatory body had to be secured. After lengthy hearings, in which mountains of briefs, evidence, case examples, and other papers would pile up, the Commission examiners would rule in favor or against the proposed move of the railroads.

Similar procedures were the rule in state public utility commissions which were empowered to rule on cases developing within the state. Thus, the railroad found itself in the position of having to run the gauntlet every time it could pinpoint specific areas where passenger train operation was piling up sizable losses daily. The ICC was described in some circles as a slow moving, detail bound agency of the Federal Government, where 560 cases were pending, some dating back to 1952. Further critics described the agency as consisting of an aged staff, hopelessly bound in an avalanche of paperwork. People were calling for an overhaul of its employees, an injection of fresh ideas and new laws. Obviously with the emerging competition of the automobile, the bus, and the airline, the monopoly and predatory practices of the railroads the ICC was set up to police had long passed. But the policing action as mandated by the public laws continued. As a result of this, a cyclic action set in with respect to passenger service. To this cyclic action was added two major factors, the recessions of 1954 and 1958

and the emergence of the highway and the air lanes as prime media of transport.

The mechanism of the cyclic action was basically simple. Since the railroads could not readily abandon their passenger trains that were losing money hand over fist, they attempted to offset the impact of these losses by eliminating certain features and services from their showcase trains. Some examples of this was the use of annoying, rasping paper headrests on the backs of reclining coach seats instead of the customary soft cotton cloth headrests, thus saving expensive laundry operations each time a train ended its run in the coach servicing yards. The operation of washing dirty windows at the midway point of the run was costly; it was discontinued. On many occasions, particularly in the winter, water for lavatories and drinking was bypassed. Coach attendant service on some of the lesser trains was superfluous; it also was ended. It was decided to discontinue the cleaning of coach interiors at the midway point of the run; they might as well run dirty until they reached the end of the trip. The nursery service on overnight trains was also too costly; it was eliminated with the result that many a coach filled with sleeping passengers on a crack train such as the *Trail Blazer* or the *Pacemaker* was awakened violently and incessantly with screaming babies and children who were either frightened, sick, or uncomfortable to the point of becoming overtired and cranky.

As a result of these economizing moves by the railroads, the once pleasurable mode of travel unveiled by the new streamliners became suddenly transformed into nine kinds of living hell. Moreover, as soon as the railroads did win approval from the ICC to drop unprofitable branch-line passenger runs, they forgot to reinstate the services they took away from the streamlined limiteds. Moreover, the courtesy of the railroad employees that was dusted off so carefully and served up to the travelling public with the new trains was allowed to slip. Reservation clerks became disgustingly surly and impatient when dealing with a passenger groping his way through an impossible-to-read timetable. Conductors treated coach and Pullman passengers as if they were some sort of plague wished upon them. In the railroad stations, a traveller could not advance fifty feet without somebody thrusting an outstretched hand in his face for some petty service rendered. More often than not baggage was lost, and a monstrous coil of red tape awaited the frantic passenger attempting to reunite himself with his missing luggage. In the dining car there would lurk snarling waiters who would become masters at the art of sarcasm if they were asked to take back sirloin shoe leather or dessert liberally sprinkled with chips of glass.

The travelling public did not have to endure abuses of services and courtesy such as they were now confronted with. As a result, the traveller left the train for other modes of travel that were now becoming more and more attractive. The silver-sided streamliners with their picture windows and their reclining seats were beginning to run with noticeably more empty seats. The trains which had received some but not all modernized equipment were running practically empty. Whatever trains had been passed over in the first round of analyses as severe money losers now became prime targets for discontinuance in the second round of analyses as to why passenger services were losing money. And so it went, cycle after cycle. The railroad managers being pure, simple, honest, upright dollars-and-cents businessmen observed that if people were not patronizing their trains, these trains were severe areas of financial losses, cast in a generally bleak profit picture for the railroads due to declining freight traffic, which was the railroads' bread-and-butter. Thus, these trains should be eliminated at all costs, but while the railroad had to go through the laborious procedures of regulatory agency hearings, it would tighten its belt on all existing passenger operations as much as possible. The travelling public on the other hand being equally pure, simple, honest, sensitive people with feelings and rational minds felt that if they were to endure a steady diet of unrealistically high fares, dirty coaches, neglected sleeping accommodations, poor food, late arrivals, and missed connections overlaid with callous, shabby, and at times downright abusive treatment by the employees of the railroad, they would bid these rolling palaces of filth a fond adieu, the better to see them from their car as they drove along the brand-new turnpikes or flew overhead in the Constellations and DC–6's of the expanding airlines.

For in the early 1950's, the "monopoly" of the railroads was indeed as alive as the dodo bird. The Pennsylvania Turnpike stretching from the Ohio to the New Jersey border carried an overwhelming load of cars day in and day out. When the New Jersey Turnpike was completed, it opened up New York City to the residents of Pennsylvania so if service on the railroad was beyond the point of endurance, they now had the alternative of driving

to New York without so much as encountering a stoplight. In New York State, Governor Thomas E. Dewey proposed a high-speed toll road linking New York City with the cities of Upstate New York, and in 1955 the New York Thruway was in full operation between Buffalo and New York, the paralleling New York Central scarcely able to raise a hand. By 1956 the Thruway had stretched to the Pennsylvania line and the completion of the Ohio and Indiana Turnpikes made it possible for Chicago to be linked to New York via a high-speed limited-access toll road. In the same year the Eisenhower Administration passed the Interstate Highway Act providing for massive Federal aid in constructing a 42,000-mile system of freeways linking the major cities of the nation.

The airlines ever since their infancy had been operating with government subsidy. These subsidies were granted by the Federal Government mainly to keep open the air mail links across the nation while the infant industry acquired enough momentum to move people swiftly from city to city. After World War II, this industry, aided by large airport expansion projects financed from Federal and local taxes, expanded by leaps and bounds. On the runways lengthened and improved with billions of dollars in public money landed 80- and 90-seat Constellations and DC-6's and DC-7's which immediately and permanently captured the business traveller away from the Pullman car. It made the businessman infinitely more mobile; now he could prepare his work in his office in the morning, drive out to the airport, transact his business 600 miles away in less than three hours, and be home again late the same evening. The Pullman at that moment became a gadfly to the traveller and to the railroads alike. The icing on the cake was the extremely courteous services the airlines rendered — from the reservationists who really seemed dedicated to sincerely caring for the traveller's best interests, to the smiling stewardesses who made the passenger feel completely relaxed. Once upon a time a terrifying experience where passengers had been required to wear parachutes, flying had now become infinitely safer than driving a car, in terms of fatalities per million passenger miles travelled. Although flying would never surpass the enviable safety record of the passenger train, its statistics were no deterrent to the thousands upon thousands of passengers who willingly abandoned the passenger train in favor of the airliner.

The railroads in the East made one feeble attempt to resuscitate their passenger service, which was staggering as a result of regulatory inflexibility, the railroads' own inept operations, and the deleterious effects of subsidized competition. This was the introduction of a series of low-slung lightweight trains patterned after the *Talgo* type trains that had been quite succcessful in Spain. The most notable of these lightweight experimental trains were the *Aerotrain* and the *Xplorer*.

Originally known as *Train X*, the *Xplorer* was frequently used as cannon fodder in the bitter proxy fight between corporation raider Robert R. Young and the incumbent management of the New York Central that had held the reins of leadership ever since the days of the Vanderbilts. Robert R. Young became prominent as a sort of maverick in the industry when as chairman of the board of the Chesapeake and Ohio he referred to Pullman cars as rolling tenements and published advertisements to the effect that a hog could travel coast-to-coast in a stock car while passengers were forced to stop in Chicago. In the proxy fight Young alleged that *Train X* would erase New York Central's $50 million passenger deficit reported in 1948.

After Young won control of New York Central in 1954, this proxy battle resulted in the present management of the New York Central, headed by Alfred E. Perlman, giving the green light to *Train X*, which assumed the name of *Xplorer*. In mid-1955, the train was ordered from Pullman-Standard, with the diesel locomotive being built by Baldwin-Lima-Westinghouse. This locomotive was a diesel-hydraulic locomotive rather than the typical diesel electric then being produced.

*Aerotrain* was a product of the same gigantic corporation that had literally sired the diesel-electric locomotive and in 1954 had seen trends which indicated that the standard-sized passenger train was imperiled unless it evolved into a radically new form. General Motors called upon its coach works at Pontiac, Michigan to construct *Aerotrain's* cars, designing the futuristic-looking diesel-electric locomotive to haul the train at sustained speeds of 100 miles per hour or better. It was advertised as the train that could save an industry, being 65 per cent less expensive to build and 60 per cent less expensive to operate than conventional passenger equipment. The Rock Island and the Pennsylvania were the first customers for *Aerotrain*, and at the same time the New York Central ordered *Xplorer* it ordered *Aerotrain* as well.

What happened to both *Xplorer* and *Aerotrain* on the New York Central was relatively sudden and swift, and was characteristic of what happened to the experimental lightweights all over the railroads of the East. It was similar to what might have happened to a baseball shortstop who had had a ground ball hit to him and a chance to make a game-winning double play, but instead let the ball roll through his legs and allowed three runs to cross the plate, causing the ball game to be hopelessly lost.

With appropriate ceremonies, ruffles, and flourishes, *Xplorer* went into service on May 16, 1956 between the cities of Cleveland and Cincinnati. On its maiden run, the train was able to reach a maximum speed of 92 miles per hour but was not able to post any sustained speeds because of road restrictions. The comfort was described as "adequate" by those that were passengers on its initial trip. *Train X's* counterpart, known as the *Daniel Webster*, went into service on the New Haven between Boston and New York.

*Aerotrain* went into service in late 1955 between Chicago and Detroit. It made the 284-mile trip in a shade under four hours, averaging 70 miles per hour. Its interiors were noisy although the seats were quite comfortable. It was described as having limited lavatory space and some extremely discomforting sideway as it rounded curves. Meals were served in the form of box lunches, and although the speed was an improvement over trains such as the *Twilight Limited*, its passengers felt generally less comfortable than in conventional equipment.

The shortcomings of both *Xplorer* and *Aerotrain* as well as the remainder of the *Talgo*-type lightweight trains could have been rectified. As with any innovation, these trains had bugs, both within the technological framework of the trains themselves and also within the manner in which they were presented to the public at large. The technological bugs such as the violent sideway on *Aerotrain* would have required modifications in design of the suspension system, but the opportunity to win back the bulk of automobile passengers in the 200- to 400-mile trip market went unheeded in the decisions not to remedy these riding inconveniences. Similarly, the lack of lounges and comfortable lavatory facilities in the lightweights was not improved upon. But most significantly, the railroads using these lightweight trains made no attempt at all to pass on to the travelling public the operating cost reductions inherent in these new trains, nor did they operate these new trains with any concerted aim towards speeding up the net travel time between the cities they served, so that the lightweights would represent the optimum means of travel between the metropolitan centers. Thus, the railroads in 1956 had had the means for retarding the exodus from the passenger trains, if not reversing this trend entirely, but they operated these trains in such a manner as to increase the shortcomings of the passenger service they were providing.

*Xplorer* and *Aerotrain* were definitely innovations, but these lightweight trains were not used to their full potential nor did the railroads capitalize on the lowered operating costs of these trains to lower the fares and thus make them serious competition for the private automobile and airline. A vigorous management might have made a serious rate case out of these new trains. Instead, the railroads took a different tack.

In 1957 New York Central made sweeping consolidations in its passenger timetable, which merged many through trains together and made connections with key trains on other railroads virtually impossible. At the same time, it filed for a 45 per cent increase in Pullman fares together with a 5 per cent boost in coach fares, making airline travel a genuine bargain compared to rail travel. By 1958, the lightweights were caught up in this overall degradation of passenger service and became victims of circumstance rather than additional reasons as to why passenger service was declining from the rails. The reasons for *Xplorer's* demise were feeble: despite a fair reception by the travelling public and a minimum of operating costs, its revenues failed to cover terminal expenses in Cleveland and Cincinnati. *Aerotrain* similarly ended its career between Chicago and Detroit with excuses belaboring the high overhead costs. The lightweights on other railroads were phased into commuter service, then vanished altogether from the rails.

The losses in passenger service continued to assume staggering proportions. In 1955 the railroads lost $700 million, followed by an almost identical loss in 1956. In 1958, on the eve of the inauguration of the Boeing 707 and Douglas DC–8 jetliners, the railroads topped their record for losses with a whopping $723 million. In 1958 came the sobering report from the Interstate Commerce Commission Examiner Howard C. Hosmer which stated that if the decline in passenger traffic continued at its present rate, the passenger coach would take its place in the museum alongside the stagecoach and the steam locomotive. The report went on to predict that parlor car and sleeper car service would vanish by 1965 and coach service by 1970. The report

then continued by stating that the commercial need for continuance of passenger service was unperceptible, and that the only advantage the passenger train had to offer over its competition was safety.

By 1958 the railroads in the East were in so serious a financial plight due to the overall economic recession that the fantastic hurdles they were forced to overcome in order to amputate their cancer-riddled passenger service by the regulatory bodies were being surmounted now with relative ease. The once-proud Great Steel Fleet of the New York Central was a virtual skeleton of its former self, with some of the proudest names in railroad history like *Pacemaker, Commodore Vanderbilt, Mercury, Lake Shore Limited, Water Level Limited, Paul Revere,* and *Detroiter* wiped out. To this roster of now-eliminated names the Pennsylvania added equally famous ones like *Trail Blazer, Red Arrow, Jeffersonian,* and *Clevelander.* Gone from the Baltimore and Ohio were names like *Shenandoah, Cincinnatian,* and *Washingtonian.* All over the East, the coaches and Pullmans were towed away to sit idle in the coach yards until such time as foul weather would tie up the roads and ground the airliners. An investment of billions of dollars now was laid to rest. Over 400 stations were put up for sale by the New York Central, ranging from the towering spire of Buffalo's Central Terminal to a small shanty which Central railroaders renovated and presented to two ten-year-old girls as a playhouse.

Like a bleeding and mortally wounded beast the passenger operations of the railroads of the Northeast staggered into the 1960's. Heavy passenger-carrying railroads such as the New Haven fell into hopeless bankruptcy. Other eastern railroads like the Pennsylvania made almost-profitable operations from their high-density passenger service in the New York–Washington corridor, but were screaming to abandon service everyplace else, including the world-famous *Broadway Limited.* The New York Central reported that the Thruway had siphoned off half of its remaining passenger traffic, and where a whole series of passenger trains had once operated between Boston and the Midwest, there was now only one.

In the face of an unprecedented period of economic growth that the United States experienced from 1947 to the 1960's, which saw the Gross National Product rise from just under $250 billion in 1947 to over $650 billion in 1965, the corresponding patronage of the railroads passenger trains fell from over 3.8 billion passenger miles travelled to only slightly higher than 17 million passenger miles logged in 1965.

The full impact of the collapse of the railroads' passenger service can be seen by comparing the statistics of the pre-Depression era of 1929 with the lows of 1965. In 1929, the railroads operated over 65,000 passenger cars of all descriptions. There were over 226,000 miles of railway in the United States where a passenger might travel by taking the train. Nearly every Class I railroad operated passenger train services. By 1965, the number of passenger cars operated by the railroads had shrunk to 10,000 cars of all descriptions, many of these still in commuter services, and 60 per cent of which were of pre-World-War-II vintage. The route-miles of coverage had shrunk to 75,000 miles where a passenger could ride the train. In 1965, the mail service carried aboard passenger trains had dropped to such an extent that the number of railway postal employees had been slashed to half of what it had been just ten years earlier. The vast marble-tiled passenger terminals, which were at one time bustling with the activity of thousands of travellers, were now virtual tombs, save for the occasional nostalgiac who wanted to ride what was left of the passenger train fleet "just for a change." And many of these railroad stations were now boarded up, demolished to make way for urban redevelopment, or else left as a prime target for the inevitable vandals. The platforms were ripped up and the rails removed to be used more profitably elsewhere.

In many areas of the country, particularly the South and the West, the vanishing passenger train by 1965 was successfully defying the predictions of the 1958 Interstate Commerce Report. Trains headed to the sunny expanses of Florida were continuing to be booked at levels of 90 per cent occupancy and higher. These trains have offered innovations such as hostess-staffed recreation lounges that would be a credit to any airline, matinee and evening movies, candlelight dinners in luxurious dining-car facilities, but above all, the courtesy and attention which despite the automobile and the jet have retained and even expanded the market for Florida services.

Similarly, the railroads serving the West have offered comparable passenger train services. Transcontinental passenger trains such as *El Capitan,* the *Super Chief,* and the *California Zephyr* have provided such innovations as dining room coupons which provide five full meals for the low rate of $12.00, ensuring the traveller a rich diet of sirloin and roast beef en route to San Francisco and Los Angeles. The railroad and sleeping car fares have been slashed on thirty-day fare bases to provide sturdy competition for the jets that are making Los Angeles practically a neighbor of Chicago. There is still a large number of passengers who evidently desire to see the country from ground level without overtaxing the family automobile. And the railroads of the West and the South are evidently doing the unheard-of thing of actually welcoming these people on board their trains, by providing them the comforts and conveniences of the passenger train — as should be.

However, in the Northeast, there are little vacation incentives such as the beaches of Florida or the wide expanses of the West. Here travel moves between cities primarily for business purposes and for personal visitations, with the exceptions of the tourist attractions of New York, New England, and Washington. In this area, the subject of this book, the passenger train has fared infinitely worse — almost to the point of passing from the scene in the manner that we have described. The result of this passenger-service collapse has had the serious effect of creating within the ranks of railroad managements of the Northeast the negative attitude that passenger service in general cannot succeed at all. Passenger service should be maintained only in areas where there is a demand for it, and in other areas, should be summarily discontinued as soon as the regulatory agencies will permit it. The fact that train travel *could* be effectively marketed and sold to the public, as the Canadian National discovered with its *Rapido* that operates between Montreal and Toronto or as the Pennsylvania witnessed on its *Broadway Limited* when it ran a very clever series of advertisements in the *Wall Street Journal* did not counteract this negative attitude.

It must be said in all fairness to the railroads of the Northeast that the immense problems of regulation and of subsidized competition did indeed play a devastating part in bringing down their once-vibrant passenger business. However, the railroads were not blameless by any stretch of the imagination. Ever since Cornelius Vanderbilt uttered those famous words, "The public be damned!", the railroads have been forced to wear the mantle of robber barons and the challenge was set for the railroads to sell themselves to the travelling public. To this they made a notable start in the wave of new streamliners which were introduced after World War II, but when declines set in, the railroads were incapable of considering any other course of action than to amputate all service they considered unjustifiable to operate, and when they were faced with constraints in this action by the regulatory agencies, they downgraded their entire passenger operation by pruning "unnecessary expenditures" whenever they felt this was needed. Unfortunately, the convenience of the public more often than not was among the "unnecessaries" when the railroads carried out these austerity programs. And instead of waging positive marketing strategy to win passengers back to the rails, the railroads bewailed the regulation and subsidized competition they had to contend with. One railroad executive commented that if General Motors had to operate in the league the railroads operated in, the huge corporation would be broke. To this it may be countered that the railroads have yet to produce on the national scene an inventive genius like Charles Kettering or a dynamic business leader like Alfred P. Sloan. The railroads had in their hands a potential weapon to compete with the automobile and the airliner in the 200- to 400-mile market with the lightweight passenger train. Cast in the general muddle the railroads' overall policy with respect to passenger service found itself in, the lightweights became as effective as a cap pistol in winning back passengers.

By default of the vanishing passenger train, the entire transportation system of the Northeast would soon find itself face to face with an ever-growing problem as the 1960's moved onward. In the meantime, in stark contrast to the inglorious retreat the railroads had made in passenger service, they were meeting a much greater challenge head-on.

The challenge was to their very existence.

A distant horn . . .
The nervous excitement of waiting . . .
The whoosh and throb of the mighty diesel . . .
The screech of brakes . . .
The glistening silver flash of the cars . . .
The stairwells being lowered . . .
The last goodbyes . . .
The "All Aboard!" . . .
The slam of doors and stairwells closing . . .
The clickety-click of the accelerating streamliner . . .
The flash of the observation car . . .
The distant drone of the diesel . . .
     . . . this was the passenger train.

In the terminals . . .

. . . or out on the main line . . .

... the passenger train had for decades stood as the living personification of the railroad in the minds of generations of Americans. If there was any single way that the railroad came in direct contact with the lives of millions of people, it was by way of the passenger train.

With the end of World War II, the railroads embarked on a prodigious modernization program designed to bring to the rails the very latest in streamlined equipment. Glistening stainless steel passenger trains made their debut everywhere to greet the travelling public.

Although the bitter cold and violent storms of winter would halt other forms of travel, it could not stop the passenger trains—and the men that operated them. The new streamliners in addition to their luxury were the most dependable form of transportation offered to the American public.

Presidents . . .

. . . and their campaign adversaries . . .

. . . spoke over the length and breadth of the land, from
the open rear platform of the passenger train . . .

126

. . . even as it raced to oblivion.

The branch-line locals were basically unable to compete with the automobile and the bus. They were operated with long-obsolescent equipment and made frequent, annoying stops of long duration for the sole purpose of servicing the local mail. As a result, they ran practically empty and the railroads made every effort to eliminate them.

128

But eliminating such unprofitable passenger trains was not an easy task. Regulatory bodies such as the Interstate Commerce Commission delayed the railroads' efforts to abandon these passenger trains for months on end. The resultant overall losses to the entire passenger service the railroads provided mounted into the millions of dollars. As a result, the railroads invoked austerity in all phases of their passenger operations. The comforts and courtesies the travelling public had enjoyed aboard the new streamliners was rapidly downgraded. Coupled with this austerity, fares were hiked to levels beyond all reason for the shabby service the railroads began to offer.

What happened next was quite predictable.

The crowds of people that once filled the passenger terminals . . .

131

. . . could now be found at the airports.

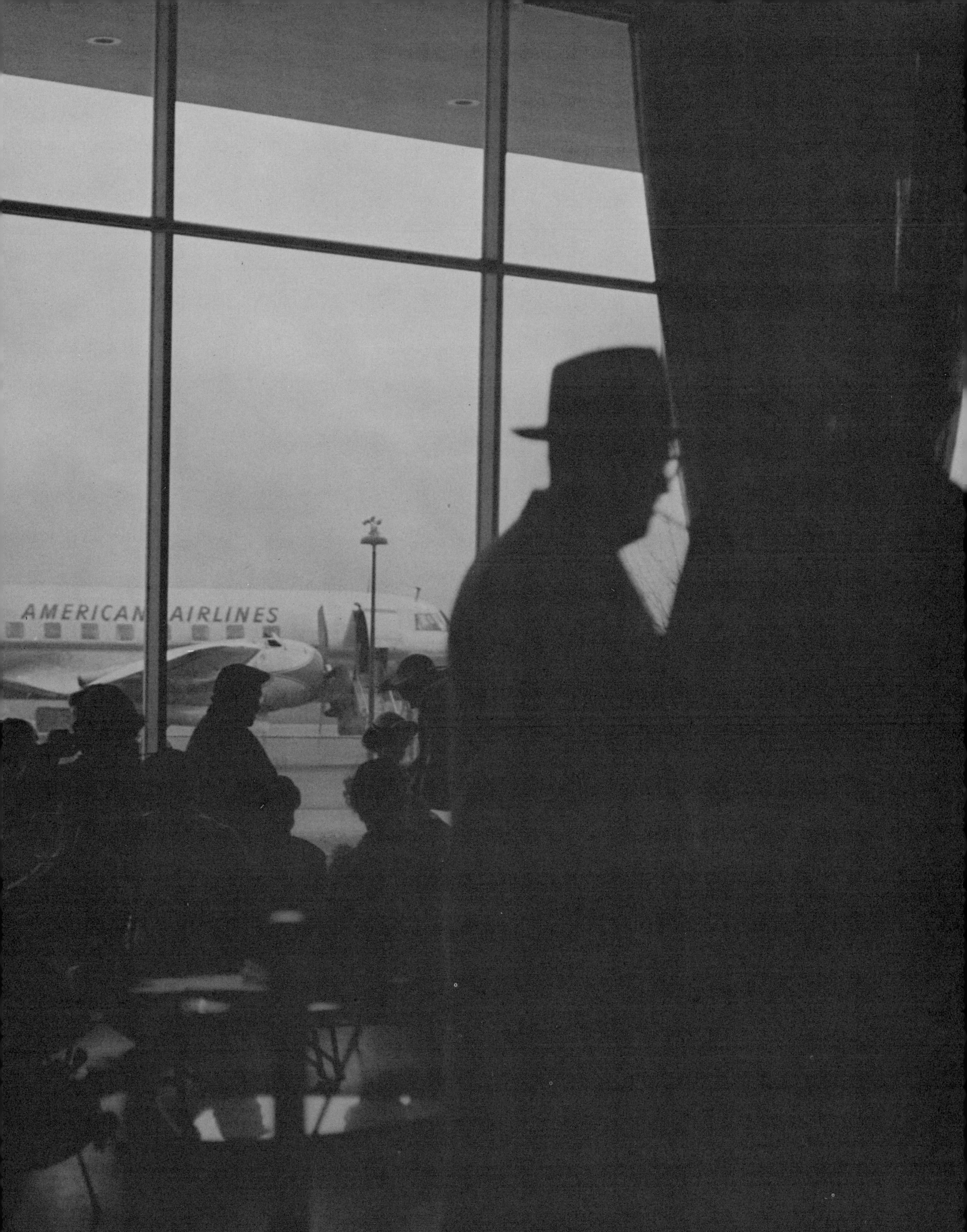
AMERICAN AIRLINES

Around the clock . . .

. . . the Convairs, the Viscounts, the Constellations, the DC-4's and the DC6's were flying through the Northeast Quadrant, creating a new travel pattern, taking the travelling public out of the crack streamliners.

And while the plane flew over the steel rails that now
carried mainly freight . . .

. . . other machines were at work building the expressways which one day would be just as congested as the
airways were now becoming.

138

The rollcall of passenger trains wiped off the schedules, began to sound . . .

*Missourian, Knickerbocker, Southwestern Limited . . .*
Gone.

*Trail Blazer, Jeffersonian, Phoebe Snow, Black Diamond . . . Gone.*

140

*Commodore Vanderbilt, Advance Commodore, Water Level, Paul Revere . . . Gone.*

*Pacemaker, Mercury, Lake Shore Limited, Clevelander,
Detroiter, Nickel Plate Limited . . . Gone.*

*Advance Empire, Red Arrow, Mohawk, South Shore Express . . . Gone.*

The proudest name in railroading, *The Twentieth Century Limited* . . . Gone.

An investment of millions of dollars . . . Gone.

In 1955 and 1956 *Xplorer* and *Aerotrain* made their debuts along with other *Talgo* type low-slung lightweight trains patterned after a similar type of passenger train highly successful in Spain.

(*Courtesy New York Central*)

*Xplorer* was touted by the late Robert R. Young as the train which could erase the huge passenger train deficits on the New York Central. *Aerotrain* was touted by General Motors as the train that could revolutionize an industry . . .

. . . both trains failed.

*(Courtesy New York Central)*

Only a skeleton force of the once-mighty passenger fleet
remained in service.

Most of these were Southern-bound, like the *Orange Blossom Special* and the *South Wind* . . .

. . . or else they were the swift streamliners that race along the Northeast Corridor such as the *Congressional Limited* . . .

But the abandoned station, the ripped out rails put to better use elsewhere, the rotting wooden platforms . . .

These stand as monuments to the vanishing train.

152

# 4

## The Quiet Revolution

By 1958 the railroads were in deep, deep financial troubles. The mushrooming rise of competition, much of it subsidized at one or more governmental levels, had bit in deeply to chop millions of ton-miles of earned revenue off the railroads. Overlaying this new competition was a severe recession which saw the Gross National Product dip from an average of $450 billion in 1957 to an average of $430 billion in 1958. The performance of the railroads in terms of net operating income had declined to a record low of $748 million in 1958 compared with over $1 billion in 1953; the rate of return on investment after depreciation had sunk to a low of 2.76 per cent. The railroads of the highly industrialized Northeast were in precarious financial condition. The combined tonnage of the New York Central and the Pennsylvania, which had come to 444 million tons in 1947, had plunged to less than 300 million tons in 1958, almost 30 per cent less tonnage than they had hauled in the pre-depression days of 1926–1929. One large road was very close to showing a net operating loss for the first time in its long, proud history. Many smaller roads were in receivership or close to the act of petitioning for bankruptcy. Indeed, the spectre of bankruptcy loomed high for every railroad of the East, and the possibility of government takeover became very much apparent for the first time since 1932, the very abyss of the Great Depression.

The picture became infinitely worse three years later. By 1961 net railway operating income had receded to its low water mark of $538 million with a rate of return on investment a meager 1.97 per cent. The railroads share of intercity freight traffic had fallen from 68 per cent in 1947 to 43 per cent in 1961. With statistics such as these, the railroads' ability to attract new capital for investment was virtually wiped out, as money could earn more invested in savings accounts than in railroad securities. The one-time monopolistic giant of the American Railroads was now classed as a dying industry. To the man in the street the railroad was definitely dead. The passenger stations were boarded-up hulks, attacked nightly by sign-writing, stone-throwing vandals. The passenger trains — what few of them were still running — were filthy rolling graveyards of metal. The freight trains were losing out, too, because everywhere one turned there were millions upon millions of trucks on the road.

But underneath this apparent pallor of death for the railroads a "quiet revolution" was going on, as New York Central president Alfred E. Perlman described it. It did not resound like a space rocket blasting off from then-named Cape Canaveral, nor did it scream by like a giant jetliner taking off from a mile-long runway built with taxpayers' funds. This "quiet revolution" recognized the vast array of serious problems that were threatening to turn the rails and the rolling stock that rode them into museum pieces, and was beginning to cope with them slowly but very methodically.

What were these problems?

First and foremost was the almost unreal position the railroads stood with respect to the local, state, and Federal governments — which possessed the power dictated by mandate of the public law to regulate and to tax. The railroads, as shown earlier, were the prime force in the forging of a new continent and the massive revolution that occurred in manufacturing, engineering, and the resultant industrialization of the United States. There was virtually no other way for people to travel or goods to be shipped. As a consequence, the railroads were creating for themselves a monopoly over transportation — and sparked by the great tycoons such as Hill and Vanderbilt, they became predatory monopolies, rife with abusive practices designed to control and restrain trade. Thus, the railroads had invoked upon themselves the stern regulatory power of a society dedicated to the preservation of free competition. By virtue of the bigness of the railroad, it also became a juicy target for taxes, these being quite easy to collect from the huge railroad empires that owned the enormous castles of real estate in the city and the miles and miles of tracks that ran everywhere through both city and country. By 1947 the monopoly was dead but the regulation and the taxes were still very much alive. These represented a strait-jacket with respect to establishing a fair competitive market price for the services the railroads performed, that of moving goods and people. It also represented a fixed tithe to be paid to the state year in or year out, whether many trains moved day and night or only one lonesome train a day wandered out on the main line. The man on the street might see the deserted railroad station as an eyesore sitting in the dirty end of town, but somebody in City Hall was collecting taxes from this piece of real estate.

While the railroads were feeling the stifling effects of regulation and the severe bite of taxation cutting into their very vitals, they were witness to the same society benignly appropriating vast sums of money for the construction of new airports, highways, and waterways at an alarming clip. It was almost like a nightmarish game of Robin Hood, who once upon a time and long ago would steal from the rich monopolistic railroads and bestow upon the poor. But then the process would keep occurring again and again until the Federal and State Robin Hood began to take from the railroad poor and bestow lavish appropriations to the benefit of the now-rich airlines, barge, and truck lines that used public roads, airports, and waterways.

While giant trucks roared day and night over the roads, pounding them into washboards of ruts, potholes, and cracked slabs of concrete, the trucking companies would pay their taxes for gasoline and licenses and that was the end of it. It would be up to the cities, counties, and states to maintain the roads and repair the incessant damage caused by the pounding trucks. The roads were kept free of snow, policed, and had their entire lengths lighted, marked, and repaired by public funds. New roads for other trucks to reduce to concrete rubble were built by the public money. The Interstate Highway Act which gave trucks a concrete high-speed main line to all points was financed by the public. The truck lines did not have to maintain the roads they travelled on or pay property taxes on the roads they used, as the railroads had been required to do; they maintained every mile of track their trains rolled over and paid a sizable amount of taxes on every mile of the same track.

The giant jetliners were beginning to be delivered — the Boeing 707's and the Douglas DC–8's. To accommodate these new airliners the existing airports had to be enlarged and expanded. New terminal facilities had to be built, including expanded parking spaces, new exotic buildings which symbolized the very concept of flight, futuristicly designed ticket counter facilities, and swank cocktail lounges where travellers could submerge their flight anxieties under several rounds of extra-dry martinis. New runways had to be built capable of withstanding the impact of tons of airplane slamming into them at over 100 miles per hour. Longer runways had to be built to allow these turbine-powered birds of aluminum to gather the necessary speed to lift their 120-passenger payloads into the skies.

But did the airlines themselves construct these jet-age facilities? Of course they did not. The counties, cities, and states again poured millions upon millions of the public funds into these enormous projects. All the airlines supplied were the jets to fly from these modern air terminals, the ground crews to service the planes, and the uniformed reservationists to man the ticket booths. At a tower high above the terminal building a shift of FAA air controllers directed the intense air traffic. County and city employees maintained the airport terminal facilities and the long stretches of runway and taxi-

154

ways. In contrast to this, the railroad supplied the men who manned the signal towers and yard classification towers. The men who maintained the miles and miles of communication lines and signal systems were railroaders. The men that kept a constant surveillance on the track and roadbed were railroaders. The men that maintained every building the railroad owned were railroaders or else worked under contract to the railroads. The public tax money subsidized and supported the facilities by which the train's competitors were able daily to siphon off the traffic the railroads could have carried cheaply and economically, drawing a share of this tax money from the railroads themselves. Without this public tax support, the competition would have had a far different base from which to match their goods- and people-carrying ability with that of the rails.

The competition for bulk freight was not confined to the highway or waterway. In 1958 a development occurred in the state of Ohio which made the coal-hauling railroads of the East swallow hard. The experimental coal slurry pipelines at Cadiz, Ohio had proven themselves. As a result, a ten-inch coal pipeline was constructed from Cadiz northward to Eastlake, Ohio, and by 1959 the pipeline was moving coal from the mines to an electric utility power company station at a rate approximating one million tons of dry coal per year. While strings of coal-laden hopper cars sat idle or rolled slowly from the southern Ohio coal fields to the lakes, the coal pipeline pulsed with its three pumping stations night and day, seven days a week. The coal slurry flowed into the electric utility's extensive drying facilities where it was de-watered, dried, and fed to the boilers of the power plant. The only significant business the two railroads were able to gather up was the lakes shipping traffic which peaked in summer and lulled in winter.

But in 1961 the railroads saw a new and vastly more ominous threat which could break the back of their entire coal-hauling operation. On a balmy June night a diesel switching crew in the coal yards south of Cadiz observed a silver-sided tank truck rumble out of the complex of buildings where coal slurry was prepared for pipeline transmission, stop for weighing on the trucker's road scales, and then continue on into the darkness down the dusty road. This was no ordinary truck. It was headed for a place called Wind Ridge, Pennsylvania where a convoy of many other tank trucks were shuttling back and forth carrying thousands of gallons of coal

slurry for a test on the twenty-four inch pipeline called the Little Inch. The experiment with coal slurry in a large pipeline between Wind Ridge and Uniontown was inconclusive but the intentions were crystal clear. A huge coal slurry pipeline from the coal fields of Ohio, West Virginia, and Western Pennsylvania was in the design stages which would carry upwards of ten million tons of dried coal a year to several large power plants on the East Coast. And three months later, the pipeline to the East Coast became a giant step closer to reality when a fleet of barges tied up at the Eastlake docks, took aboard one million gallons of coal slurry and transported them to a power plant at South Amboy, New Jersey, where for thirty days a test was conducted which burned this million gallons of coal slurry as if it were crude oil. Whatever the state of the railroads' declining markets, the bleak year of 1961 was a mild dream compared to the hideous nightmare the railroads would face if their coal transport market were suddenly lost to a network of coal slurry pipelines.

If bulk commodities such as coal were in danger of being lost to the railroads, the shipments of finished merchandise were already lost. In the shipping of merchandise, the railroads considered this as Less Carload, or LCL. This term indicates that not all the cubic footage of the car was taken up with the commodity being shipped as opposed to, for example, a box car filled with grain or a tank car filled with chemicals. Merchandise shipping was slower via rail than truck, because trains invariably had to be classified and reclassified a dozen or so times from the time the manufacturer loaded his goods aboard the boxcar until the consignee received and unloaded the goods. Moreover, the loading and unloading of merchandise presented problems. If the originating shipper or the destination were not on a railroad siding, the goods had to be loaded aboard a truck, unloaded at the freight forwarder's warehouse, loaded aboard the boxcar, unloaded at the destination warehouse, reloaded aboard a truck, and then unloaded at the consignee's premises. Damage in transit was not the exception; it was the rule. It was far, far simpler to ship by truck over the highway. And many, many merchandise shippers did just that. The problem was so basically simple: the boxcar could not go where there existed no railroad siding, and it was slow going traversing the infinite delays in the classification yards of the railroads.

Automobiles were another case. Here the railroads had historically provided wide, double-door boxcars for the movement of autos. The automobiles had to be painstakingly loaded aboard these boxcars to avoid damage, and only four vehicles could be put aboard these cars. Like the problems in movement of less-carload merchandise, the automobile cars found themselves mired in the railroads' classification yards, with a sizable inventory of automobiles always in transit between the assembly plants and the distribution points. To the automobile manufacturer there were two solutions for reducing this inventory held up in transit — either decentralize their assembly plants or else ship by truck. They did both. As a result, parts movement from fabrication to assembly plants became a critical factor in their manufacturing cycle, but the costs of inventory were lowered by use of motor transport. Something else was also lowered. The 60 per cent of all automobiles manufactured which the railroads once hauled was shrunk to a dribbling 10 per cent.

The railroads were at wits end to cope with another problem as well. This was the fantastic relationship with the operating Brotherhood unions that represented engineers, fireman, brakemen, switchmen, and conductors. These craft unions were to a man highly independent, proud organizations of men highly skilled in their trade, and just as highly bent on keeping the *status quo* very much intact. It was not only the loss of jobs due to technological change which these unions feared; it was the extinction of their very unions as well. Work rules remained intact no matter what the technological change would otherwise dictate. Two-way radios had to be supplemented by hand signalling. A road crew could not switch cars off their train in the yards; a yard crew had to do it. But most of all, a fireman still had to be part of the locomotive crew aboard a diesel with no steam whatsoever and no coal to shovel. The railroads wistfully observed that no less than $200 million could be saved annually by elimination of the fireman aboard diesels. But in the meantime, their operating costs continued to rise.

However, the quiet revolution was working at the same time the railroads were incurring this resounding economic thumping. The railroads were waging a meager advertising campaign pleading for equality of competition, but with the public having had negative experiences aboard the passenger trains, their sympathies could not be so easily evoked. However, when railroading, especially in the East, began to approach crisis level, a faint glimmer of daylight was observed to be coming from Washington. A Presidential Advisory Committee on Transport Policy was set up in 1955. The resultant report took cognizance of the fact that there had occurred a revolution in transportation and that the virtual monopoly the railroads had held on intercity transportation had ceased to exist. Citing the wide selection of transport modes available for goods and people, the report concluded that the government *still* viewed rails as a monopoly, which had resulted in dislocations in the nation's overall transportation system costing the general public $1 billion a year or more. By 1958, when the railroads' plight had become acute, the Smathers Subcommittee on Surface Transportation had generated bills in the House and Senate which created loans up to $700 million, guaranteed by the government, for necessary capital improvements to the railroads. The bills also created some reforms in the regulatory policy of the Interstate Commerce Commission.

In 1960 a staunch spokesman for the re-establishment of equality in competing modes of transport was elected to the Presidency. In each State-of-the-Union message to Congress, President Kennedy stated that the current laws were a legacy from an earlier period and while the need for regulation continued, technological and structural changes today permitted greater reliance on competition within and between modes of transportation. The specific recommendations were for elimination of Interstate Commerce Commission authority over minimum rates for agricultural and bulk commodities, imposition of charges for commercial use of publicly provided transportation facilities, and increased expenditure of Federal funds for transportation research. In 1963 omnibus bills were introduced in Congress, mainly to eliminate authority of the ICC in establishing minimum commodity rates. As of the present day, the legislation completely freeing the railroads from establishment of minimum rates has not been enacted, but Federal aid has been coming in ever increasing amounts for transportation research. The establishment of the Northeast Corridor experiment and the inception of the turbine-powered train have been evidence of this increasing support to restore the glaring unbalance of our national transportation system.

In a message to Congress on March 2, 1966, President Lyndon B. Johnson stated:

156

America today lacks a coordinated transportation system that permits travellers and goods to move conveniently and efficiently from one means of transportation to another using the best characteristics of each.

With this came a request to Congress to establish a Department of Transportation for, among other things, coordinating the principal programs that promote transportation in America, bringing new technology to a total transportation system, and to encourage high-quality, low-cost service to the public. For the first time, a concrete proposal to remedy the imbalance of the nation's overall transportation system had been espoused. In October, Congress passed the legislation creating a Department of Transportation, and by 1966's end, Alan S. Boyd had been appointed by President Johnson to head it. Seemingly, the railroads stood to gain much from creation of this new Federal department, in terms of research and development of even greater technology for the purposes of moving goods and people.

However, the one millstone which had hung over the railroads for so long — the Interstate Commerce Commission with its onus of crippling regulatory practices — had not been taken into account either in the formation of the Department of Transportation or in the future views of the new Secretary of Transportation. The ICC, the Civil Aeronautics Board, and the Federal Maritime Commission were not included in the initial proposal for the Department of Transportation. They were not made a part of the Department when it was finally legislated into being. And in the press conference which Mr. Boyd was confronted with immediately after his appointment, he stated that he did not favor having the ICC eventually moved into the Department of Transportation, and almost at the same time went on record as favoring the granting of motor carriers the right to operate trucks of greater length and weight.

Based on this, the creation of the Department of Transportation holds out potentially little immediate hope for the railroads to regain their respectful economic place in the sun. Interstate Commerce Commission regulation has been a Gordian knot in the railroads' efforts to provide economically feasible transportation to shippers and passengers alike. By ignoring the vital regulatory aspects associated with our transportation system, and particularly the railroads, the Department of Transportation was in effect undermining its mission, as ordained by President Johnson, of encouraging private enterprise to take full and prompt advantage of new technological opportunities as well as of encouraging high-quality, low-cost service to the public.

If the railroads were relatively unsuccessful in winning basic freedoms to establish unregulated lower rates through legislation, they were much more successful on winning several key issues on lower rate establishment either through the proceedures of the ICC itself, or through action of the courts that were called upon to hear the cases. The railroads were able to sharply lower the differential between conventional boxcar rates and the new Trailers-On-Flat-Car (TOFC), the latter being decided in the Supreme Court. In a unanimous decision in April 1963, the first opinion interpreting section 15a (3) of the Interstate Commerce Act, the Court said:

. . . if there is one fact that stands out in bold relief in the legislative history of section 15a (3), it is that Congress did not regard the setting of a rate at a particular level to constitute an unfair or destructive competitive practice simply because that rate would divert some or all of the traffic from a competing mode.

The battle was being joined on other fronts as well. In the classic battle to establish a 60 per cent saving to shippers on grain shipments from the Mississippi and Ohio River crossings to the South and Southeast, the Southern Railroad overcame Interstate Commerce Commission restraining orders via the courts. The wave of favorable court decisions was instrumental in making the ICC vacate an order requiring rail–ocean differentials on movement of steel pipe from Official Territory (the East) to the Southwest.

Thus, like an army advancing through a fortified enemy line, pillbox after pillbox of resistance to the railroads' ability to move commodities and merchandise cheaply and competitively were being overcome. The frustrating regulatory constraints were being loosened gradually by a concerted legal action which the railroads were employing. The legal staffs of the railroads were a new breed unlike the real-estate and claims lawyers found in railroad corporate headquarters in the monopoly days. Young aggressive lawyers well-versed in antitrust legislation and trade regulation, these men must take credit for laying the groundwork for the major advances the railroads were able to bring about, even if the required legislation for complete emancipation from regulatory constraints in minimum rate-making was yet in coming. Ultimately, it would come, but in the meantime, the railroads' aggressive legal action in getting lower competitive rates established was beginning to pay off.

But how does one go about establishing a lower rate for the finished goods and merchandise which must be loaded, unloaded, classified, and stored so many times, while the truckers have a field day siphoning off this goods movement from the railways? The answer goes back a long, long way into railroad lore.

One of the most colorful trains to come into town was the circus train. It would steam into town with gay yellow supply wagons, bright red carts with lions in their cages, huge green stage wagons, smaller silver tent wagons. It was almost like a fairyland processional, but it all rolled by train aboard flat cars with their wagons and vans specially anchored so that they would not roll off due to the jolting and lurching of the train. The circus train would ease into the siding, teams of horses would be backed up ramps leading up to the flat cars, the wagons would be rolled off, and the parade would start through town. Indeed, the circus came to town on piggyback.

Piggyback . . . the name had a ring to it. If the circus could move by train and parade so gaily through town on its way to the fairgrounds, which were near no railroad siding at all, why couldn't the long ponderous trucks which ground through town have their trailers put up on flat cars piggyback style? It was an idea, and one worth trying without many development costs attached to it. The railroad had many many flat cars and it wasn't long before the railroads were offering piggyback service on an experimental basis to selected off-track customers. The idea caught on very rapidly and by December of 1954 almost all the railroads save the New York Central were using Trailer-On-Flat-Car (TOFC), which was synonymous with piggybacking, on many of their freights. By March 1955, TOFC had become big business when on an evening in Chicago a three-unit diesel backed into a solid mile-long train of trailers on flat cars on the Pennsylvania Railroad yards and moments later was roaring eastward to Philadelphia with TT–1, the first all-TOFC merchandise freight. By April, the Pennsylvania's Truc-Train service was approaching 500 trailers per week. In all of 1955, over 168,000 flat cars containing two trailer vans each were loaded with TOFC traffic. By 1963, this

figure had risen to slightly under 800,000 cars loaded in that year. Despite the plunging statistics in overall freight traffic the railroads were reporting, TOFC traffic ascended to new heights, indicating one basic fact to the railroads that had never before been established more clearly. It was simply this: the railroads must provide a service tailored to the customers' needs of moving commodities and merchandise cheaply — without damage or excessive handling, and with efficient speed from origin to destination. The customer would not adapt his needs to what the railroad would supply. This maxim was being proven by the long silver TOFC trains which cut carloading and handling costs to the bone, and brought back tons and tons of merchandise traffic that otherwise would have been lost to the highway.

On the New York Central, a further step in piggybacking was developed, again by simple reasoning and logic. In operating a TOFC service, why was it necessary to expend diesel horsepower to pull such dead weight as trailer tires, plus the heavier flat cars required to support them? In 1957 this railroad had answered this question by developing a containerized van-on-flat-car system where each flat car, with two pivotal turntables, could receive a container which rolled on its rear trailer wheels over the road. When the container was backed up and attached to runners on the turntable, the rear trailer wheels were detached and the container was pushed further onto the turntable. The container was then pivoted to line up parallel to the rails. Two such containers could be transported on this specially-equipped flat car and the New York Central's Flex-i-Van service was thereupon inaugurated.

Thus a new concept was unveiled — Container On Flat Car (COFC). COFC had additional features such as the containers' ability to be transported aboard ocean-going vessels to foreign port cities and thereupon trucked to their final destination. Since the New York Central more than any other railroad was affected by the St. Lawrence Seaway, it was this railroad's answer to competition — overnight delivery from the Midwest to the port cities, then transfer to ships without incurring handling damage, pilferage, or any of the other ills associated with the transfer of goods at the waterfront to the ships at sea. COFC also halted the flow of lost bulk mail transport from the baggage and mail car system of movement to containerized vans that could be loaded and unloaded at any post office.

In 1965 the New York Central had alone moved a high of 122,000 vans in its Flexi-Van service; by 1966 this figure was well on its way to approaching a quarter of a million such units. It was sufficient to win the President's "E" award for the unique way it cut costs, time, and pilferage in exporting goods overseas.

Thus with Flexi-Van and TOFC service, an explosion had occurred in the intercity movement of goods and merchandise. The railroads, moreover, had a long, long way to go in reaching their ultimate potential for TOFC and COFC services. Where the truck lines were finding that they, in turn, would be subject to increasing road taxes, labor charges, and fuel costs in operating their truck-trailers over the turnpikes and highways, the railroads, which could move 200 to 300 such trailers in a single train, now had the advantage of vast untapped capacity at relatively little cost increments. And therefore, the Flexi-Van and TOFC terminals were expanded almost on an annual basis. The Pennsylvania's Kearny Yard near Newark, New Jersey, which handled 11,000 TOFC trailers a month, was undergoing its third expansion since 1955 — and undoubtedly more would follow. As Churchill remarked after North Africa had fallen to the Allies in World War II, "We cannot say that we are at the end, or even truthfully say that we are at the beginning of the end. However, I believe we can cautiously say at this point that we indeed are at the end of the beginning." In like manner, the railroads could not say that they were in the process of sweeping every truck-trailer off the roads, but they could say that TOFC had stopped the loss of intercity merchandise to the trucks and indeed was making a modest reversal of the trend.

If such reversals of the trend could be made with piggyback, were not such gains possible with the virtually dead market for intercity automobile transportation? All the railroads had in 1958 were their four-car automobile boxcars to move their miserable 10 per cent share of automobiles from assembly plant to market. The answer to the question of how they might win back this lost market came from Europe, where in 1955 the British offered a passenger service of shipping automobiles along with their passengers. The Germans in 1958 paraded out of their Volkswagen plants double-level flat cars which hauled these beetles, ten to the car, to the port cities of Hamburg and Bremen for export to the United States and other lands. The American railroads had experimented with various rack cars which were no more than open-sided versions of the conventional boxcar. However, the railroads seized the German concept of multi-level rack cars in 1959–1960, finally developing a standard 85-foot-long, tri-level rack car capable of hauling twelve Cadillac-sized sedans or fifteen Corvair-sized compacts. The railroads wound up and let fly with this new development in 1960, and soon one of the most breathtaking sights the casual train-watcher would ever see would be the onrush of a six-unit diesel with car after car of beige, maroon, and acquamarine Chevrolets, Dodges, Mercurys, Oldsmobiles, and Ramblers streaking over the crossing, making a wild blur of chrome and color as the train seemed to glide over the land with new cars for the showroom. While the automobile manufacturers welcomed this new mode of travel, the truckers most certainly did not. At one stage, bands of vandals would station themselves with acid atop railroad overpasses to drop their deadly chemicals on these automobile trains until a combination of railroad police riding shotgun aboard the trains, local police, and the FBI put this sabotage to a quick end. Despite these initial incidents, the railroads were at the end of 1966 again knocking on the door of the former 60 per cent of the automobile transport market. The New York Central alone hauled over 1.1 million automobiles in 1965, 12 per cent of the nation's production. At present, ML–12, a daily three-mile-long solid multi-level train of fully assembled automobiles is operated by this railroad between midwestern assembly plants and eastern terminals. The Pennsylvania matched this production by moving well over a half-million automobiles in the same year. The problem of stuffing four assembled automobiles inside an antiquated boxcar was over.

But what about that coal pipeline network that by the end of 1961 was threatening a solar plexus blow at the railroads' bread-and-butter traffic? The railroads formed their first line of defense in the state legislatures, for here was where the coal pipeline in order to become a reality would have to secure the rights of eminent domain in order to cross private and corporate property. Since some of this corporate property was the rail network over the East, the railroads marshalled their lobbies in the legislatures of West Virginia, Maryland, Pennsylvania, and New Jersey for a last-ditch fight. The results were not long in coming. In Ohio, the pipeline already had the right of eminent domain and was day and night pumping millions of gallons of coal slurry to Eastlake. In West Virginia, a state with vast coal mining interests depressed from the late 1950's, the right of eminent domain was awarded to the pipeline project. In Pennsylvania, a state also with vast coal mining interests but one where the railroads had also many friends, a titanic hammer-and-tongs battle flowed back and forth in the legislative halls of Harrisburg. When the smoke of battle had cleared, the eminent domain legislation had failed to pass, but not by much. The railroads had held. New Jersey and Maryland were anticlimatic, and here as in Pennsylvania the eminent domain legislation had failed to gain enough support to become law. The railroads breathed a sigh of temporary relief, for without this legislation there would be no West-to-East pipeline. However, there would always be another try at this legislation, and this time the railroads might not fare so well. As in everything else, the best defense was always a good offense, and the railroads soon had their offensive weapon. This was the unit train, a train consisting of solid hopper cars which would be loaded at the mine and moved at high speed to the electric utility plant, unloaded rapidly, and then moved at high speed back to the mine for a refill. The rates for coal hauling would be slashed drastically, being established by contract rather than on a coal-car-by-coal-car basis. Trains of the railroads' best and biggest hopper cars were assembled and in mid-1962 were shuttling back and forth between the mines and the power plants who by this time were looking favorably at this cost reduction the railroads were able to give them immediately, without recourse to a new nuclear plant costing many millions of dollars or to a pipeline which might take at least three to five years to become fully operational.

At the same time, the railroads prepared the knockout blow to the one existing coal slurry pipeline. They proposed unit train service from Cadiz, Ohio to Eastlake on a rate which yielded a healthy profit to the railroads and still undercut the combined cost of pipelining the coal slurry up to Cadiz and at the same time maintaining the expensive dewatering and drying facilities at Eastlake. The utility company was very receptive to this reduced-rate offer from the railroads, since the year before it had been forced to withstand a cyclone of protest from the surrounding townships of Timberlake, Eastlake, and Wickliffe. In attempts to upgrade the concentration of coal from 50 per cent to 60 per cent in the slurry, the finely powdered dry coal had created problems in feeding it to the furnaces, which had on occasion emitted heavy black gobs of coal slurry which would rain over the landscape, after being carried by the winds blowing off the lake. On other occasions, sparks would fly from the smokestacks, creating numerous brush fires. But most of all, the sixty-odd jobs required to maintain the drying and dewatering plant could be abolished by the utility company. Thus, in the spring of 1963, the pipeline was mothballed, and the drying plant at Eastlake sat as a silent monument to the greatest threat the railroads ever faced and overcame — while the unit trains of coal rolled along into the unloading pits nearby.

The unit train concept spread to other areas of railroading, all achieving the same effect of bringing about sizable rate reductions with bulk handling of commodities. Grain unit trains moved from the wheat fields to the grain elevators. From the steel mills of Lackawanna, a unit train of flat cars moved with hot steel slabs to the rolling mills of Burns Harbor, Indiana. Alumina moved in solid unit trains. So did iron ore. The quiet revolution was rolling.

But what powered these new trains that made the freight train of the 1950's so poor by comparison? The answer was in the third-generation diesel-electric locomotive that was as different from the diesels of the early 1950's as these were in turn from the steam locomotives they replaced. The general-purpose diesel, or road switcher came into widespread prominence in the mid 1950's and had helped to finish off the last of the steamers as well as create a new trend in diesel utilization. By 1955 the streamlined freight diesel had been dropped from the line of products by all major locomotive builders, and from there onward development was based on upgrading the general-purpose locomotive. The horsepower per unit of road switchers climbed to 1750, then to 2000, as developed in the GP-20 by General Motors which was placed in service by 1960. In addition, the road switchers took on a characteristic new look with the low-profile hood, which allowed the engineer much the same visibility over the road he had with the streamlined F-3's and F-7's, but also retained its general-purpose characteristic in that the crew could have both fore-and-aft visibility as in switching locomotives. Thus the 1960's saw the introduction of the third-generation diesels with 2500 and 3000 horsepower per unit. General Motors continued to produce the lion's share of these locomotives, along with Alco Products (once the American Locomotive Company) and a newcomer — General Electric. This latter manufacturer had been associated with the locomotive business in many ways all throughout the 1950's, building small switchers, teaming with Alco to provide traction motors and electrical generation equipment for that manufacturer's line of locomotives. In addition, at its Erie works, General Electric had built impressive lines of pure electric locomotives. In 1963 a new line of diesel-electric locomotives began to roll out the doors at Erie which found rapid acceptance by the railroads. Called the U-25, this low-profile unit packed 2500 horsepower generated by Cooper-Bessemer diesel engines and transmitted to the rails by a new alternator-type electrical generator and AC-DC electrical transmissions.

By 1965 the low-profile diesels were beginning to replace the scores of older F-3 and F-7 freight diesels and some of the not so old Alco road switchers and General Motors GP-7's. Two new diesels could do the work of three older ones. Freights reached new lengths of 200 to 250 cars, all of which could roll at speeds up to 70 miles per hour. Maintenance was slashed to the bone on these new locomotives. In terms of rising labor and fuel costs, these factors did not affect the third-generation diesels. In 1966, General Motors announced the most powerful line of diesels ever built. There were nine models of locomotives in this line with horsepower ranging up to 6000 in one unit. These had new traction motors designed for the heaviest as well as the swiftest of freights. A four-unit combination could work a TOFC overnight merchandiser at sustained speeds of 80 to 85 miles per hour and come back the next day at the head of or else cut into the middle of a 300-car coal unit train. General Motors had built a new diesel engine — the model 645 — to replace the 567 which had been utilized since 1938. In addition, the six-axle, six-motor diesel which boasted horsepower up to 3600 was being ordered by the railroads in their third-generation diesels. The move was for power and for even further reduced operating costs — and the locomotive builders had come through.

Because of the great visibility and non-maintenance-on-line of low profile diesels, the railroads finally concluded that the fireman was absolutely usless in these new machines and represented millions of dollars going down the drain in the name of featherbedding. In November 1959 the railroads demanded work rules changes dealing with elimination of the firemen from all freight and yard diesel locomotives. A crisis appeared imminent, finally resolved with the establishment of a Presidential Railroad Commission to investigate the work rules problem and report it in 1962. The Commission in 1962 reported what the railroads had felt all along — that the firemen were non-essential in yard or freight service. By November 1962 the problem had risen to the Circuit Court of Appeals who upheld the District Court's decision that railroads have authority to impose work rule changes, and thus paved the way for the case to go to the Supreme Court. In March 1963 the Supreme Court upheld that the railroads did have the right to make work rules changes.

The railroads immediately shot the gap, announcing changes would be immediately forthcoming. The threat of a paralyzing strike seemed certain, halted only by President Kennedy's action in creating a temporary emergency board which cut off the hiring of new firemen and made provisions for the termination of existing firemen of less than ten years seniority. In August 1963 a seven-man tripartite arbitration board was created to dispose of work rules issues. The famous Arbitration Board Award 282 provided for the gradual elimination of 90 per cent of freight and yard fireman's jobs, with benefits for those so displaced. In April 1964 Arbitration Board Award 282 was upheld by the Supreme Court, and for two years thereafter the railroads were able to eliminate freight and yard firemen in states not covered by full crew laws. In 1966 would come a strike on certain railroads whose unions were attempting to reinstate the lost jobs — but as 1966 ended, the featherbedding issue had been tackled and won. The impediments to technological progress were being knocked down, one by one.

The technological progress was also responsible for carving huge chunks out of the exorbitant volume of operating costs the railroads had to pay to maintain their miles and miles of track. Welded rail cut down track wear. New defoliating agents reduced the problem of weeds and grass growing over the roadbeds. But perhaps the greatest gains were made by Centralized Traffic Control, or CTC.

At a control panel in Erie, a two-man crew sat before a huge illuminated board which displayed every mile of track, every switch, and every signal between the Buffalo and Cleveland terminals of the New York Central. Colored lights indicated the location of every train on the line. Along the entire stretch of track at seven-mile intervals a series of high-speed switches were constantly under fail-safe control, switching high-speed trains around slower trains, enabling the two-track main line to carry more traffic at higher speeds than the old four-track main line could do before the advent of CTC. The financial rewards were quite evident. The taxes saved on the reduction of trackage went into the millions of dollars, as well as the reduced maintenance on these unneeded stretches of main line.

Other aspects of modern technological improvement were use of two-way radios between locomotives, cabooses, and control towers. Brakemen in the yards could communicate with switching crews and with the yardmaster's offices and control towers by two-way pocket radio. The classification yards which at one time were flat expanses of track with rows upon rows of cars sitting idle, waiting their turn to be made up into trains bound for their final destinations were also modernized. In 1966, huge ultramodern classification yards such as Frontier, Conway, and Gateway worked night and day handling up to 5000 cars per day, utilizing automatic car weighing devices feeding information to tireless control computers that assigned tracks, setting switches for the endless parade of cars to roll down gravity humps, and operating car retarders to halt the speed of these cars rolling down hill so that there would be no damage to their contents. Other sensing devices pulsed at electronic speeds feeding car number identification to other computers over leased telephone lines so that other men by pressing a button and looking into a TV-like device called a Cathode Ray Tube could see information pertaining to cars, trains, and locomotives displayed on the screen.

Indeed, the "quiet revolution" had come. The railroads in 1966 were able to report record earnings and healthy financial status, a completely different picture from the monetary depths they had reached in 1961. The 1965 annual reports of the two largest railroads in the East showed average consolidated earnings of better than $6.00 per share. In 1966 the intercity freight traffic of the railroads reached 745 million revenue ton-miles, a figure that topped the all-time high of 737 million ton-miles set during World War II. The net earnings of the railroads rose to $930 million, representing a healthy rebound from the dismal days of 1961 when the railroads stood at the brink of disaster.

Despite this startling reversal of performance, the railroads recognized that this was posted in the greatest economic boom the country has experienced. Moreover, one statistic which still stared the railroads in the face was the fact that where they had managed to just exceed their 1947 levels in terms of ton-miles hauled, the trucks carried over four times

their 1947 levels, and the oil pipelines and water carriers were at least 1.5 times over their 1947 levels in terms of ton-miles hauled. Also of note was the fact that the New York Central and the Pennsylvania combined had not managed to even approach the total tonnage levels they were able to haul in the years 1926 – 1929. The TOFC trains, tri-level automobile rack trains, and unit trains had arrested a long and serious decline, and even reversed the trend in some areas. The railroads by means of the quiet revolution had achieved much, but there was a long uphill road ahead to climb. Moreover, the nagging question has persisted as to how the performance of the technologically-oriented railroads would look if there were an economic reversal. This question became very much apparent during the first quarter of 1967 when there was a decided economic slowdown from the booming year of 1966. The high leverage inherent in railroad operations once again became a dominant factor in projecting earnings for the railroads. Additional traffic, in keeping with an economic boom, or more desirably, a shift in transportation patterns away from competing modes of transport to the rails, does not require compensating increases in manpower or other operating costs. On the other hand, a decline in traffic over the rails brought about by an economic slump or loss of tonnage to competitors can shrink profits to dangerously lower levels. The railroad costs in the main have been stable, unaffected by peaks or lows in traffic, but subject to critical upward pulling forces such as rising labor wages, rising taxes, and rising costs of fuel and services rendered to the carriers. The new technology has been able to aid immensely the profitability of the carriers in the 1960's by holding if not lowering this fixed cost outlay by the railroads. Now, since the economic picture in the first half of 1967 has indicated a slump, the railroads have found the necessity for additional rate increases to offset decidedly lower earnings projections for the year. Of even greater necessity was the need to further lower the level of fixed costs of railroad operations. The most promising means of accomplishing this appeared to be by combining services which were presently being duplicated by one or more paralleling railroads or else being rendered inefficiently as a result of existing operating practices which could be combined much more efficiently under a single management. Obviously, this meant merger. To this aim, the railroads had long been at work.

In 1958 the New York Central and Pennsylvania

had astounded everybody when, in the depths of financial crises, they had sought merger as a way out of their difficulties. Since then, there has been a general pattern of mergers forming in the railroads — both Eastern and Midwestern. The most notable to date have been the Baltimore and Ohio with the Chesapeake and Ohio which gave the B & O a transfusion and restored it from the ranks of the sick to a profitable operation. The B & O has retained its separate identity but many services and features are combined with those of the C & O to the extent that numerous areas of duplication have been eliminated. The Norfolk and Western has combined with the Wabash and the Nickel Plate to form a system extending from Roanoke, Virginia to Omaha, Nebraska. But the merger of the New York Central with the Pennsylvania would have the greatest impact on the entire transportation system of the Northeast. The possibilities for such a merged line were, to say the least, exhilarating. The world's largest transporter of merchandise and bulk commodities would come into existence with an unduplicated road of steel rails extending from the Midwest to the huge marketing areas of the East as well as to the port-city gateways to the world. Here solid unbroken COFC and TOFC merchandise trains would flow at speeds approaching 100 miles per hour with no classification yard delays whatsoever in the entire journey. The price of this service would reflect the economies of scale now made highly attractive by the wholesale elimination of costly duplication of services so that traffic would bounce back to the railroad, revitalizing this industry on a scale so vast as to make the previous cost improvements petty by comparison. The car interchanges between the systems amounting to 600,000 cars a year would be wiped out. A joint committee of New York Central and Pennsylvania executives estimated that transit time over thirty-three routes would be reduced up to 38 per cent. Pooling of duplicate terminal facilities of the two roads would be saved in eliminating duplication of passenger train operations, but this is low considering what potential profit would be developed by the innovation of the new high-speed passenger trains now under experimental development. The merger, then, would allow accelerated and improved service, yield an astounding cost reduction, and utilize all the technological tools developed in the "quiet revolution" — the new diesels, the containerized van shipments, the unit train, and last but not least, a new breed of manager well versed in engineering technology, operations research, and management science.

It remained for the two railroads to weigh all the positive merits of a merger during the next four years. In April, 1962 the roads filed formal application for merger, and it was not until April, 1966 that the Interstate Commerce Commission gave approval to the merging of the two railroad systems. However, the Erie-Lackawanna, fearing that it would become isolated in the formation of the large rail systems of the Northeast, filed suit along with other smaller railroads equally concerned in becoming included in one or the other of the major railroads being created by merger. The Supreme Court was called upon to hear the case, with the result that in March, 1967 it ruled that the merger could not take place until the ICC found a place for the three smaller railroads — the Erie-Lackawanna, the Delaware and Hudson, and the Boston and Maine. The problem of absorbing the bankrupt-ridden New York, New Haven, and Hartford had already been resolved prior to the Supreme Court decision. The ICC responded in June by indicating the three smaller railroads were to be included in the Norfolk and Western system. The Norfolk and Western, its eyes set on merging with the C & O — B & O system, had no plans to take in the three railroads until after this merger with the larger system had been consummated. On June 13, 1967, the N & W filed suit challenging the ICC order that it acquire the three smaller lines, following this up with a request to the Federal District Court to block the Penn-Central merger until final court determination of the ICC order had been resolved. The net result of this court maneuvering thus has delayed the formation of the Penn-Central system, with the two railroads faced with the continued inefficiencies of parallel operation, duplication of services, and elevated base operating costs incurred as a result. The railroads of 1967 could ill-afford to be obstructionists in the paths of their fellow railroad systems' efforts to wipe out operating inadequacies via consolidation, for their competitors that rolled over the highways were themselves becoming more efficient. The trucking lobbies were making two- and-three trailer over-the-road units realities on the turnpikes and freeways of the nation, turning them into nightmares for motorists to negotiate. In order for the balanced transportation system to survive, the railroads must continue to offer services to the shipper at rates designed to attract traffic to the rails, and only by maintaining or lowering the fixed costs at steady or declining levels could this be possible.

It was imperative that this balanced transportation system be maintained, especially in the highly populated and industrialized Northeast, for the Jet Age and the Turnpike Age had now entered into a new problem caused by their own spectacular growth.

The airways and roadways were reaching the danger point of congestion. And people once again were beginning to look to the rails.

The beginnings of the 1960's saw the railroads of the Northeast in the worst financial plight of their long history. The competition from the trucks, barges, and pipelines had captured millions of tons of freight from the steel rails, leaving the freight train to seemingly plod along an uncertain path with now only a minor share of intercity goods movement.

The freight trains droned onward past the many railroad stations that were now abandoned, never to see service again . . .

. . . as whatever passenger trains that still were running only drew the attention of a solitary baggage cart or an occasional little boy as a spectator.

But at the same time, there was also occurring what railroaders would conservatively call, " a quiet revolution." It would be a technological change almost as startling as dieselization had been. Huge truck trailers and entire fleets of band-new automobiles would speed along piggyback style on flat cars, pulled by the most powerful diesel locomotives ever built. Solid unit trains would revolutionize the delivery of coal to the user, slashing costs to new low levels. Sophisticated electronic control systems and computers would cut days off the time it formerly required to move goods from shipper to destination.

A new dynamic era in railroading had begun.

Perhaps the idea of piggybacking started with the circus train, perhaps it originated from some other source. However, the movement of trailers on flat cars immediately became big business on the railroads, halting the bleeding off of merchandise traffic to the truckers. The multi-level automobile rack car was capable of hauling 12 full-sized sedans or 15 compacts. It restored to the railroad the leadership in the transport of new automobiles to the showroom.

170

To pull these new swift trains, the third-generation
diesel made its debut. Characterized by a 2500-horse-
power turbosupercharged engine, an AC-DC alternator,
and a low profile nose, these machines were as revolutionary as the original diesels that had driven out the
steam locomotives a decade earlier.

172

The piggyback freight trains moved like crack express trains. Shippers were given printed schedules, and railroaders were instructed to give these trains top priority in their movement. By day and by night, these trains rolled . . . fast.

The concept of piggybacking was extended to the transport of the automobile from assembly line to showroom. Formerly hauled aboard double-door boxcars, this type of car became so inefficient a means of hauling automobiles that the railroad's share of the auto transport market dropped to a dismal ten percent. Developed in Europe, the multi-level rack car was an instantaneous success in enabling the American railroads to win back the major share of the movement of automobiles from the assembly plants to the new car buyers.

175

During the early 1960's when freight traffic sagged badly on the railroads during the recession period, piggybacking managed to increase year after year. It finally spearheaded a marked reversal of the ebbing flow of traffic, to where in 1966 the railroads carried over a million piggyback units.

The Pennsylvania and the Baltimore & Ohio specialized in hauling truck trailers on flat cars (TOFC). Another piggyback concept was called Containers-On-Flat-Cars (COFC), or Flex-i-Van, by the New York Central, which developed it.

Let us take a look at the New York Central and its fleet of Flex-i-Van freights in the freezing grip of a typical winter on the Great Lakes . . .

179

In a setting of bitter cold and blowing snow riding the crest of high winds off Lake Erie, crack Flex-i-Van freights pause momentarily in their 16-hour dash to the East Coast.

180

Even the mail and express goes Flex-i-Van. Once restricted to the baggage cars of an earlier era, the containerized mail now can go right to the Post Office door . . . indeed, in the dead of winter, the mail does go through.

In no other imaginable setting can the dependability of the railroads be so well described as that of a typical Lake Erie winter. Where sheets of ice coat the roads and white waves of snow reduce visibility to zero, the trucks cannot operate. The frozen canals and ports have stopped the barges cold, literally. The ocean-going freighters that ply the Great Lakes are safely tied up in port.

But where everything else stops under the spell of winter, the railroads go.

The railroad is well-equipped power-wise to handle the worst that winter can offer. The latest and most powerful four-axle, four-motor machine in the long line of general-purpose diesels from Electro-Motive, the GP-40 awaits the "clear" signal with a Boston-bound Flex-i-Van containerized freight.

The men must keep the trains rolling through the worst
of the snow and the cold, whether to climb high atop
the hood of a diesel to repair an air horn or to refuel
a four-unit 12,000 horsepower locomotive at the head
of a Chicago-bound Flex-i-Van freight such as the LS-1.

All this, before the full fury of a blizzard blows off the lake . . .

The business of railroading went onward as the savage onslaught of winter mellowed into spring and summer. For the first time in a decade, the railroads were beginning to experience some measure of prosperity. No doubt much of it could be attributed to the boom years, but the "quiet revolution" had enabled the railroads to move much more merchandise and freight at operating costs that were holding the line against rising prices. With savings being passed on to the shippers, the freight was beginning to return.

188

In Ohio, a coal slurry pipeline was pumping over 1 million tons of coal a year from the mines to an electric utility power plant. The prospects for additional pipelines looked imminent. The railroads had to meet this new competition — quickly. They put their new powerful diesels at the head and in the middle of trains consisting of brand-new coal hopper cars, and rolled them at high speeds, shuttling between mine and user. The unit train, 200 to 300 cars long, acted like a pipeline on wheels as it made no other stops than to change crews between origin and destination. The cost savings in operating the new diesels and elimination of all yard switching were passed on to the user, making the unit train more financially justifiable than operation of the coal pipeline.

The one operational coal slurry pipeline in Ohio was shut down in 1963. The unit train had won another victory in the "quiet revolution."

The "quiet revolution" was not only confined to the piggyback express freights or the unit trains. It also brought the electronic age to the railroads, from two-way radio communication . . .

. . . to elaborate sensing and control devices tied to giant computers which created a new concept in speeding *all* freight to its destination — this was the giant, electronically controlled classification yard.

Here over 5000 cars a day move in continuous processions over gravity humps to be classified into trains bound for their final destinations. Automatic sensing devices have identified each car by number, and automatic weighing devices have determined each car's precise weight. From devices such as these, information flows in electronic pulses to giant computers which assign destination tracks to the cars now being uncoupled manually. These computers also control track retarders which, based on the weight of the car, slow it down to an exact speed designed to avoid damaging its contents in colliding with other stationary cars on the receiving track. The computer also feeds information to the locomotive dispatchers who get the powerful diesels ready for the flood of trains due to leave these mammoth classification yards. The weight and destination of each train are known so that the right power combination will be ready at the right time.

Twenty-four hours a day, seven days a week, the mammoth classification yards operate. The days of the slow freight, another relic of the past, have all but ended. Yards such as Conway, Gateway, Potomac, and Frontier have slashed days off the time required to deliver freight.

By day, the yard is a beehive of activity. By night, it is a wonderland of sights and sounds, illuminated like twenty football fields and throbbing with activity across every mile of its many tracks.

At the same time men are working to move the long trains through the classification yard, other men are working to keep the diesel locomotives in proper mechanical condition so they can move out to the ready track, to await the call to roar through the night with crack trains of piggyback freight or automobiles headed for the dealer's lot.

Men sit at control panels with lights winking and flashing, controlling the overall operations of the yard . . .

198

. . . as car after car moves over the humps in never-ending processions over the vast expanse of yard, bathed in brilliant floodlights.

And thus, the "quiet revolution" continues onward. The electronic age will give more benefits to the railroads, now fully aware of what they can yield. The powerful low-profile diesels will continue to pull two-mile long trains of automobiles and coal at express train speeds, someday reaching 100 miles per hour.

However, there is one frontier left. This last frontier of the "quiet revolution" is anything but quiet. The new technology has given the railroads the means to consolidate their operations, forming larger and more efficient systems out of many small competing ones.

For the true competition in the Space Age is not railroad against railroad, but railroad against the highway, the waterway, and the air lanes.

The Baltimore and Ohio had joined with the Chesapeake and Ohio, with the result that the B&O, staggering in deep financial problems was able to undertake needed modernization as a result of the economies of merger. The Wabash and the Nickel Plate Road had merged together with the Norfolk and Western to create a system extending from Omaha to Roanoke.

However, the biggest merger of them all was now in the making . . . . .

206

The Interstate Commerce Commission had given approval for the two largest railroads in the East, the New York Central and the Pennsylvania to merge. The resultant merged system would slice untold millions of dollars a year in duplicated operating costs and inefficiencies off the budgets of the combined system. The resultant system would provide the means for the most efficient system of ground transport that the Northeast has yet to experience.

On January 18, 1968 the Supreme Court gave the final green light to the Penn-Central merger, thus marking a fitting climax to the "quiet revolution," one that has seen the railroads evolve from a cobwebbed, archaic past into a vibrant new industry.

# 5

## The Road Ahead

While the railroads were busily developing and implementing centralized traffic control, the TOFC piggybacks, the tri-level automobile cars, and the rugged new diesel-electric locomotives to pull them, the competition was also forging ahead by giant steps. More powerful truck tractors were being built so that on the New York Thruway, for example, they could pull two fully loaded trailers in tandem. The automobile had evolved into a luxuriously-styled vehicle powerful enough to cruise effortlessly at 80–85 miles per hour — when the highway patrol was looking the other way. The DC–8 and the Boeing 707 jetliners had new smaller sister craft such as the Boeing 727 and the Douglas DC–9. The giant C5A military transport was in engineering and development stages. Over 150 huge Boeing 747 jet airliners capable of seating 400 passengers were on order. The supersonic transport (SST) was in development in Britain and France, with the United States finally settling down upon a Boeing variable-wing design powered by new General Electric jet engines. The American people were getting ready to accept concussion-like sonic booms as a part of their daily existence, all in the name of progress. Thus, the quiet revolution on the railroads was not outstripping competing revolutions in other fields of transportation. It was at best merely keeping pace and allowing the railroads to partake of the phenomenal economic growth of the soaring sixties, perhaps even gaining some ground in the specific areas of automobile transport and containerized merchandise shipment.

But while this quiet revolution was taking place, and the competition was matching this revolution by continued technological advances, another process was occurring at the same time, the tremors of which were already becoming felt.

In December of 1960 there occurred a disaster of the first magnitude in the skies over New York City when a DC–8 jetliner collided with a Constellation; both aircraft had been attempting to enter their respective holding patterns to land at New York International Airport and at LaGuardia. The Constellation plunged in flames into Staten Island, fortunately out of the way of any large residential areas. The DC–8, an engine and part of a wing shorn away, swooped low over Brooklyn and crashed into a heavily residential area, narrowly missing a school with over 1700 children attending class. For three days the newspapers, radio, and television flamed with the news of this catastrophe while the prayers of a nation rang out in vain that an eleven-year old boy, the sole survivor of this mid-air collision, might live. The intensive investigation which followed this tragedy yielded much to improve the air traffic control over high-density flight areas, yet in 1965 another midair collision occurred over southern Connecticut involving a Constellation and a Boeing 707. In an unprecedented chapter of heroism in the skies, the Constellation glided to a forced crash landing in northern Westchester County with a loss of only four lives, while the Boeing 707 limped into Kennedy International Airport with half a wing torn off. And, in the spring of 1967 a brand-new DC–9, minutes away from a scheduled landing in Dayton, Ohio crashed into a smaller private plane flying by visual see-and-be-seen rules on a clear, sunlight day, killing all aboard.

Thus, the menace of aerial collision still existed despite five years in which to develop new radar tracking devices, improved communication between pilot and the ground, and the use of billionth-of-a-second giant electronic computers to predict, plan, and guide air traffic movements. The reason for these collisions has become quite plain: the skies over our nation's metropolitan areas have become so crowded that the giant four-engine jets and the smaller two- and three-engine jets whoosh and scream and thunder much like a flock of pigeons circling around a church steeple. The analogy ends at this point because the pigeons can quite well take care of themselves; the jetliners require men with unfailing nerves and the most sophisticated electronic gear with 100 per cent reliability to guide these giant birds in for safe and secure landings at the rate of one or two every minute.

Indeed, the Northeast Quadrant, which is the setting for the photographs in this book, contains the most dense air traffic patterns of any region on the entire planet Earth. The situation, moreover, is not improving due to effects of the new technology but is deteriorating so rapidly that the airlines, riding the crest of an unprecedented boom in air travel, are headed for a moment of truth, much like the man who built an expensive boat in his basement too large to ever get it out to the water.

The sky overhead appears limitless as we view it from the ground. However, the skies as the airline pilots must fly it are organized in finite, identifiable flight paths and holding patterns classed by altitudes as well as geographic reference. Identification of all aircraft flying in these air lanes as well as holding patterns is made by radar. The altitudes, air speed, and direction are reported by each pilot to the ground controllers who assign each plane definite altitudes and holding patterns in guiding the planes in to their final approach. However, adequate separation must be maintained between aircraft, due to the calibration of the radar scopes which may show variances of as much as fifteen miles around each radar blip that appears. In addition, the streams of destructive air turbulence caused by the jet aircraft knifing through the air at speeds up to 600 miles per hour causes a danger zone trailing twenty-five miles back of the jetliner in which no other aircraft dare enter. A DC–7 leaving Kennedy International Airport entered such a danger zone created by a Boeing 707 on its approach to the holding pattern and crashed off Long Island. Hence, each radar blip on the air traffic controller's scopes represents a moving block of airspace thirty miles long, about fifteen miles wide, and 2500 feet thick associated with each jet in the crowded skies. The airways are becoming congested to the point where the spaces above the large metropolitan areas are reaching critical levels.

In 1966 the expansion plans of the Port of New York Authority to build a fourth airport in Morris County, New Jersey, met a thumping defeat at the hands of landowners, conservationists, and others who were unwilling to hear the twenty-four-hour a day, seven-day-a-week thundering and screaming of the giant jetliners. Thus, the extremely difficult problem besetting the New York area with respect to its air accessibility came no nearer to solution. The three commercial airports of Newark, LaGuardia, and Kennedy were handling close to thirty million passengers a year and over a million landings and takeoffs. Moreover, all three airports are stuffed geographically within a thirty-mile radius, and as a result a fantastic series of holding patterns has been put into effect to handle the flights that come to New York from points as distant as the West Coast, Europe, and Asia or points as close as Boston, Philadelphia, Hartford, and Albany. In other cities such as Boston, Chicago, and Washington the picture is much the same — that of incredible congestion in the skies over metropolitan airports, delays in landing, and delays in takeoffs. A phenomenal dis-economy in operation of jet aircraft exists as a result, with thousands of pounds of jet fuel being needlessly consumed as long queues of aircraft await takeoff clearance or circle endlessly in the stacked holding patterns awaiting their turn to land. It was estimated during one study of such delays that the airlines were socked close to $4 million at one major airport alone as a result of airport congestion.

For once, the railroads were not alone in bewailing their plight in terms of the obstacles encountered in movement of passengers. The airline executives now began to wring their hands in dismay. Unlike the railroads, who were calling for equal opportunity to compete and were not harping too much on the need for Federal aid, the airlines were screaming for increased Federal aid to the airports and to the air control centers to reduce the congestion over the airports which has at times resulted in up to 3000 airline passengers being held in aircraft circling through holding patterns. And some of these calls from the airline executives for increased Federal aid has ironically been aimed at aiding the development of high-speed trains in the heavily-traffic-density areas and the 200- to 500-mile trips which occur in these areas. The critical point has indeed been reached when one form of transport begins to plead for assistance to a competing form to solve the overall problem.

If the skies overhead were being plagued with overcrowding along the air routes and the air spaces over the metropolitan air terminals of O'Hare, Kennedy International, and Washington, then the roadways in the heavily travelled Northeast were in far worse plight. The networks of freeways, expressways, and turnpikes were becoming paralyzed with ten- and fifteen-mile long queues of automobiles attempting to reach their destination. On the Pennsylvania Turnpike on any good summer weekend major delays were inevitably encountered in the six tunnels carrying the road through the Allegheny Mountain ridges. There have been incidents of equally long backups of traffic at the Thruway toll barriers around Buffalo and at the Tappan Zee Bridge. But this congestion is tame compared with the hardening of the arteries the road system is experiencing in the metropolitan areas of New York, Washington, and Chicago. Here traffic inches its way along roadways like an army of beetles hopelessly stuck to flypaper, with a miasma of gasoline and oil fumes rich with carbon monoxide and other pollutants rising up over the entire setting. At a speed of 70 miles per hour, a lane of highway can handle about 1000 to 1200 cars per hour depending upon average weather conditions and normal separation between vehicles followed at this rate of speed. However, if more than 1200 vehicle trips per hour are loaded onto a given arterial link, congestion develops, starting at the point where traffic leaves the link and continuing down the length of the link until the entry points are unable to admit any more cars. Then other links similarly congest and the resultant massive traffic jams are not allevi-

ated until the volume of cars demanding entrance to the system falls below the rate at which the system discharges vehicles to their final destinations. Assuming an average of three passengers per vehicle, under normal circumstances about 3600 persons per hour can be transported. However, in peak traffic periods, the roadway system capability falls below its potential movement rate of 3600 persons per hour owing to this congestion. On the other hand, the railroads have been estimated to have a potential person-carrying capacity of 45,000 people per hour.

The initial solution was to unfold the extensive files of planning studies, set up traffic counters, and call in the designers and draftsmen to plan, design, and supervise the construction of yet even more freeways and expressways. Thus, the bulldozers and other monstrous pieces of earth-moving machinery roared and scraped and dug and scooped out new ribbons of concrete. What happened was enough to confound even the most stout-hearted of the many of individuals that believed that new highway construction was the absolute cure-all.

Because it wasn't.

As the new highways were built to take traffic off the existing ones that were so badly overtaxed, they attracted new developments along their routes to such a degree that these new roadways were just as plagued with almost insolvable congestion as the previous routes had been, almost as if a hideous practical joke were being played. The only apparent solution to the congestion along the new expressways was to build even bigger expressways to relieve it.

However, there began to spring up a growing "freeway revolt" in that many people were becoming apprehensive that one enormous apron of concrete would be one day laid down to connect the growing metropolitan areas that were fusing together into one enormous supercity. The maps began to show solid blobs of area designated as supermegalopolises. The stretch from Boston to Richmond was one such supercity. The area from Syracuse to Chicago engulfing cities such as Pittsburgh and Youngstown was another. Somehow, somewhere, our mobility which we had so much taken for granted was becoming hopelessly lost.

What confounded the issue even more with respect to new highway construction was the increasing costs required to build such new expressways. Considering the viaducts, tunnels, and cut and fill required, the costs of a limited-access highway would generally average $5 to $7 million per mile.

Worse yet, each time a new superhighway was built, valuable tax-bearing land was removed from the tax rolls, the burden to be carried by the remaining taxable real property. Still worse, the establishment of a new route resulted in the carving up of neighborhoods, farms, and other natural region-forming systems. In one incidence of a "freeway revolt," a vehement protest was made on the grounds the proposed route would create a segregated neighborhood, with a Negro area on one side of the route and a white area on the other. In still another case, a year-long battle was fought between a state highway department and a planning agency over the location of a section of the Interstate Highway system; the resultant choice of routes left 1000 families as potential refugees to be relocated into new dwellings in the name of highway progress.

However, there is nothing quite like the feeling of independence an individual gets when he becomes an intercity passenger behind the wheel of his car. He has such conveniences as air conditioning, stereophonic FM radio, wall-to-wall nylon carpeting, reclining bucket seats, a car body as solid as a church, and a 390 cubic inch dipslacement engine that can tear up the road at 80 miles per hour or better while scarcely exerting itself. The fact that the individual is losing $1000 per year on the depreciation of his vehicle or that he is devoting a full fourth of his income to his automobile in terms of payments, insurance premiums, tire and battery replacements, and gasoline costs does not dissuade him from becoming a portion of the 90 per cent of intercity travellers that use the car.

Also having little restraining effects are the gory statistics the motorist manages to post each year. In 1965 over 49,000 Americans were killed on the highways, more than fell during the entire American campaign in France from D–Day to V–E Day. On a good vacation weekend it is not uncommon to have 600 or more Americans killed on the highways. The toll in human lives, in human misery, in pain, suffering, and death is immeasurable; not to mention the millions of dollars spent annually in personal injury and property damage claims. And with the ever-increasing congestion of our highway system, the grim totals rise unerringly each year.

Hence, a growing national crisis is at hand. The degradation of the railroads' passenger-carrying facilities has exacerbated the overall problem of our transportation system. Instead of growing with the rising trends of intercity passenger travel, the passenger train has become the skeleton we have described in Chapter 3. Fortunately, the passenger train has not become the museum piece the Interstate Commerce Commission examiner's report foretold for it in 1958. However, this type of passenger train will not be the answer to the paralyzing problems of our airways and roadways, mostly because of its high operating costs, high maintenance costs, and inherent 60-mile-per-hour slowness. We have seen also how lightweights such as *Xplorer* and *Aerotrain* failed due to their spartan ride, excessive interior noise level, and token improvement in speed, with no corresponding fare reductions to compensate for these inconveniences. We have also seen how these trains were downgraded in the process of the massive retreat from passenger service the railroads of the East made in the late 1950's. Yet, the problem of our deteriorating transportation system became acute to the point of concern of President Johnson and Congress. What *was* the solution? How were other people in other nations coping with *their* transportation problems? What could *we* do to alleviate our own massive problem that had been allowed to progress unchecked during the 1950's to the now-acute stage?

In the mid 1950's a series of the most spectacular tests of railborne equipment ever witnessed was conducted on the French National Railways. The *Societé Nationale des Chemins de Fer Français* ran tests to prove the effect of extreme high speeds upon locomotives, cars, and existing roadbed. In 1954, the tests began, using the normal 1500-volt DC power supplied from overhead electric wire and a standard electric locomotive with three standard coaches. The experimental train covered 23 miles in a shade over 12 minutes, start to stop, hitting a top speed of 151 miles per hour. Precise recordings of wear were taken using piezo-electric quartz and cathode tube oscillographs. The speed was measured by chronometer and tachometer.

One year later in 1955 the French repeated these experiments with other conventional electric locomotives such as used on *Le Mistral*, a crack train which operated between Paris and Lyon averaging 80 miles per hour over the 318 miles separating these cities. In this series of tests, a locomotive pulling three standard coaches established a world speed record of 207 miles per hour and thus the possibility was confirmed that the passenger train could operate much faster than most conservative railroaders would expect them to.

However, the most startling venture into the realms of high-speed railborne passenger transportation was made by the Japanese. The Japanese had the problem of congestion not only of their roadways and air routes but of their rail traffic as well, principally on the lines between Tokyo and Osaka. In 1957 the Japanese National Railways established a Tokaido Trunk Line Study Committee to find a solution to this congestion of the Tokaido route, as it was called. Among the reports of this committee were: a) that an entirely new line should be built to 4'-8½" track gauge (which is the standard track gauge operated in the United States and Canada); b) that the New Tokaido Line should be operated with commercial 60-cycle electric current and would employ multiple-unit electric railcar trains rather than locomotive-pulled trains; c) that the line should be designed for high speeds with no grade crossings or other obstructions.

Utilizing the facilities and staff of its Railway Technical Research Institute, the Japanese National Railways undertook a broad scale research and study on some 173 design problem areas, such as air pressure effect through tunnels with high-speed trains, automatic train control, braking, and traction motors. The delivery of the trains commenced in April, 1964; and by late July the track and electrical power systems were complete over the Tokyo to Osaka route, followed closely by the completion of the signalling and automatic train control systems. By October, just before the start of the Olympic Games in Tokyo, the New Tokaido Line was in operation, and a new chapter in railway passenger movement was written.

The 320-mile distance between Tokyo and Osaka was conquered by the blue-and-white *Hikari* bullet trains in 3 hours and 10 minutes, including one stop midway at Kyoto. No less than 43 trains were operated daily over this line initially, and one month later, this had been raised to 55 round trips daily. This speed record is comparable in the United States to travelling from the Loop in Chicago to the Cleveland Union Terminal in 3½ hours, or from Pittsburgh's Golden Triangle to Philadelphia's 30th Street Station in the same amount of time. Thus, the high-speed passenger train passed from the experiments of the French to practical, everyday operation, 55 times a day.

The *Hikari* trains whiz over the New Tokaido Line with the last word in modern technology. The motorman or engineer is overridden by automatic train control in decelerating and braking; he can, however, start and accelerate the train so long as he is permitted by automatic train control to do so. In the cab of each train are continuous indications of

maximum permissible speed, restrictive track conditions, and provisions for receiving coded ATC signals from track circuits along the way. A control installation at Tokyo provides for centralized train control showing visual indication of the location and number of every train on the line.

The roadbed utilizes continuous welded rail and pre-stressed concrete ties. The rails are fastened by double elastic type fastenings along with rubber track pads and springs to absorb lateral thrust and impact. The trains pass over this roadbed without the slightest indication of clatter, sway, or lurching. Completely air conditioned, the cars provide excellent comfort in the first-class sections, seat second-class patrons 3-and-2 style as in many airline coach configurations, and provide excellent dining facilities.

The results of the New Tokaido Line have been a resounding success. The trains are 92 per cent occupied on the average. Congestion on the routes between Tokyo and Osaka has been cut, and the Japanese National Railways is now thinking of extending the line via a series of inter-island tunnels from the island of Hokkaido in the north to the southern island of Kyushu, as well as achieving the overall goal of connecting the line with every major Japanese city. The popularity of these *Hikari* trains has avalanched Japan to such an extent that an advertising agency for one brand of Japanese cigarets had passed up entertainment stars and airline captains for endorsement posters in favor of New Tokaido Line trainmen. Truly, the breakthrough in rail passenger service had come to the far islands of Japan.

But what of the congested Northeast Quadrant of the United States, with its choked highways, overcrowded airways, and by contrast, deserted railway passenger coaches?

In 1964 as part of the Kennedy legacy, President Johnson had won Congressional approval of a program to promote high-speed ground transportation. Where the Japanese had invested the equivalent of $1 billion in its New Tokaido Line, the appropriation here was only a modest $90 million stretched over a three-year program. Yet, under this program, the Pennsylvania Railroad placed a $20 million order with the Budd Company (the same builder that had produced the *Pioneer Zephyr*) for advanced high-speed passenger equipment to go into service between New York and Washington by early 1968.

These high-speed, self-propelled rail cars will represent the first speedup of rail passenger service between the nation's capital and the metropolis of

New York in over thirty years. The cars will draw on overhead electric power already existing on the rail route. Like the New Tokaido Line, the cars will be designed for speeds up to 160 miles per hour, accelerating to 125 miles per hour in two minutes and reaching top speed in over three minutes. The cars will be permanently coupled in pairs and can be operated in trains up to 20 cars long. Two classes of service will be provided: parlor class and coach class. The cars will provide more interior room than standard coaches, with parlor cars able to seat 34 passengers each in individual revolving and reclining chairs. The coaches will allow their passengers to relax in wide, high-backed individually reclining seats. The cars will be heated electrically, have no-draft air conditioning, wall-to-wall carpeting, and abundant luggage space. The noise level inside is designed to be about the same as that of a modern executive office.

While the cars are designed for 160 mile-per-hour speed, it is highly doubtful that they will be operated at that speed initially unless substantial modifications to the roadbed are made. Curves which are wide and sweeping will have to go, grade crossings and crossovers of other railroads will have to be eliminated; and automatic train control to decelerate and brake these ultra-fast speedliners will have to be installed. Most probably they will see initial service at 110 miles per hour or so. Even with this, the new streamliners represent a potential new direction in passenger travel that even the lightweights such as *Xplorer* or *Aerotrain* could not reach.

Meanwhile on the flatlands of Indiana and western Ohio, yet another step was reached in enabling the sorely-deteriorated passenger train to stage a comeback. The New York Central rummaged around through its car yards, found a thirteen-year-old Budd RDC (rail diesel car) that once had served Boston and Albany as part of the proud Beeliner fleet. The diesel engines were disconnected from the trucks, and two General Electric J-47 turbojet aircraft engines that had once seen service aboard a now obsolete military aircraft were mounted atop the roof. On one end a long sloping nose was welded on which old-time Central railroaders swore had come off the streamlined front of the steam locomotive once used to pull the *Commodore Vanderbilt*. Studded in this streamlined front were two window slits that had served as number boards on an old Electro-Motive F-3 freight diesel. Special cylindrical tread wheels were installed, the nose was painted black, the New York Central emblem was slapped on, and the M-497 rolled out of the shops ready to duplicate the French experiment of eleven years earlier: to test the effect of ultra-high speeds on truck and roadbed maintained at normal standards.

On July 23, 1966, people who lived along trackside between Butler, Indiana, and Stryker, Ohio heard and saw a veritable apparition. They had heard the sound of jet aircraft and some may have looked upward, but the skies were clear. Along the track, however, like a jet fighter roared the M-497 at a record 183.85 miles per hour, leaving behind it a solid trail of dust, and a whole host of doubts that had once claimed that high speeds were impossible over existing roadbeds. The M-497 also planted the kiss of death on the remainder of the worm-eaten New York Central passenger train fleet, for on the heels of this successful jet railcar experiment came a New York Central press conference announcing an intent to petition the ICC for abandonment of all existing passenger train services, replacing the trains with newer high-speed shuttle-train service between 80 cities paired for this type of service. The service would be frequent, and the speed would be eminently competitive with air and highway transportation. Thus, what had been theory was now unmistakable fact: the passenger train in the present conventional form deserved to disappear because it was too slow, too expensive, and most of all too inadequate to compete with the jetliners, and the expressways. Moreover, because of this inadequacy, our entire transportation system, especially in the Northeast, was in grave crisis due to the chronic overcrowding of roadways and skyways.

If the conventional passenger train deserved to disappear, it could at least be said that many, many people would still ride it provided that it could offer something. An example of this is occurring in Canada on the line between Toronto and Montreal. Here the Canadian National operates the *Rapido*, a conventional coach and parlor car train drawn by a standard E-8 passenger diesel. There is no differentiation between railroad equipment operated in the United States and that operated in Canada. The track gauge is the same, and car building, both freight and passenger, is standard between the two countries — as is the case with the locomotives which are built by U.S.-owned subsidiaries. Hence, the *Rapido* would be no different in appearance between Chicago and Cleveland as it would be between Toronto and Montreal. But here the similarity ends. The Canadian National has eliminated all intermediate stops, cutting the running time to five hours flat between the two cities. Fares have been reduced to the point where the first class fare is two-thirds that of economy coach fare aboard the airlines. Most interestingly, before these innovations, the Canadian National was experiencing the same blight as the American railroads were going through. The *Rapido* has since been running 90 per cent full, and the Canadians are now marking time while *Rapido* continues to earn profits until the day *TurboTrain* enters the Montreal–Toronto service.

The American railroads — especially the bankrupt-ridden New York, New Haven, and Hartford — are just as eagerly awaiting *TurboTrain*. For *TurboTrain* represents a giant step beyond the New Tokaido Line equipment presently revolutionizing train travel in Japan and the electric-powered self-propelled cars scheduled for service between New York and Washington. In fact, *TurboTrain* may conceivably be the ideal optimum weapon by which the imbalance in the overall passenger transportation system in the East may be finally corrected.

The Japanese have invested over $1 billion in establishing a new roadbed free of curves, as well as establishing electric catenaries and power distribution facilities to propel their *Hikari* limiteds. The Pennsylvania requires a significant curve-elimination project on the New York to Washington line to enable its new railcars to exceed the 120-mile-per-hour mark. Indeed, 125 miles per hour seems to be the economic sound barrier for operation of the high-speed trains although top speeds approaching 200 miles per hour are technically within reach. The costs of making track and roadbed improvements appear to rise exponentially with respect to increasing the sustained speed of trains between cities. Furthermore, the tracks that serve passenger trains also must serve the freights — and such modifications as superelevating or "banking" the curves for operation of the high speed passenger liners would cause the slower freights to tip to the inside of the curve, risking possible derailment, or at best, aggravated wear upon the lower rail due to the shift of the center of gravity and the "bowstring" effect observed when a long heavy freight is rounding a curve.

The *TurboTrain* indeed is designed to operate well within these cost constraints, which based upon the historic attitude of railway management toward even much lesser outlays for passenger service are very, very real. *TurboTrain's* prime mover is a gas turbine engine weighing only 250 pounds, but rated at 550 horsepower. It is able to be installed in any number aboard the train, thus providing unrestrained flexibility in terms of supplied power. Hence expensive electrification is not required to operate *Turbo-Train* in non-electrified railroad routes. Coupled with this power plant flexibility is the light weight of the train, its power plant, and its components, together with the streamlining throughout the train designed to reduce aerodynamic drag present at speeds above 80 miles per hour or in operation against headwinds. Finally, elimination of double axles used on conventional railborne equipment has added to markedly decrease the resistance load of the train.

The unique suspension system has been designed to avoid the violent sidesway on curves inherent in the lightweights such as *Talgo* and *Aerotrain* as well as the punishing ride conventional train passengers have long been exposed to from vertical and lateral forces. The *TurboTrain* suspension supported from above provides a pendulum action which causes the car body to bank inward on curves much like an airplane. Together with a center of gravity only 40 inches off the rail, more comfort and speed on existing track conditions is possible, allowing *Turbo-Train* to operate on curves at speeds 40 per cent greater than conventional trains.

But comfort of ride is not all. The passengers in the lightweight trains of the 1950's were subject to spartanized conveniences and interior comfort, while the unfortunate souls condemned to ride conventional passenger coaches found themselves aboard a rolling pigsty. *TurboTrain* interiors are designed to resemble that of jet airliners, with spacious reclining seats, individual arm rests, carpets, drapes, and air conditioning which allows smokers the freedom to exercise their habit while not infringing upon the discomfort of the non-smokers. As in the jetliners, prepared meals or snacks served on seat-back tables will be available. In addition, raised dome lounges allowing a commanding view over the landscape will serve cocktails aboard these 160-mile-per-hour speedliners.

In the spring of 1967 yet another concept of railborne travel was unveiled that held the promise of enabling the vacationing traveller to relax as his passenger train sped to its destination, while at the same time allowing him to enjoy the use of the family automobile once having arrived there. Initiated by the Department of Commerce, the auto-on-train concept designed by Sundberg-Ferar, Inc. was unveiled at the Smithsonian Institution in Washington in conjunction with the founding of the Department of Transportation. Planned are a series of trains operating between Alexandria, Virginia and Jacksonville, Florida in a twelve-hour schedule over the Atlantic Coast Line route. Automobiles will be carried in double-decked cars 85 feet long accommodating four autos on each level. Driven aboard through long clamshell doors and anchored next to broad, tinted windows, the automobiles themselves would serve as private compartments by day and sleeping quarters at night. Aisles beside the automobile will lead through the carrier cars to a carpeted, double-decked lounge and dining facility car located at each end of a 12-car express. Each service car would seat 95 in its dining, lounge, and observation facilities. The lower decks of the service cars will house kitchen and dining areas, while the upper decks will provide rest rooms, a lounge area, a recreation area, and an observation deck. Additional rest room facilities are designed for the carrier cars at mid-train, emphasizing the train's service to family groups and especially those with children.

Thus, there exists a means to bring down the perplexing problem to our overall transportation system. Coupled with the astounding revolution the railroads have made in the technology of moving merchandise and commodities, the railroad of the immediate future is indeed a far cry from the railroad of 1947 with its gargantuan smoke-erupting steam locomotives and its nineteenth-century regulation and modes of operation based on a day long past. The advent of the diesel was the first step in the great transition, and the resultant economic peaks and valleys of the 1950's sparked the quiet revolution which has given rise not only to new operating methodology and innovations such as piggyback and centralized traffic control, but also to a new breed of manager who could apply the tools of engineering, operations research, marketing management, and legal trade regulation and analysis towards making even greater breakthroughs in the new railroad of the late 1960's.

The future holds much for the railroad in transition — a transition that although painful and still unresolved in a number of areas, can still be considered as a major triumph. For this transition came about in the face of almost nightmarish regulation of the railroads by governmental bodies while these same governmental bodies were channeling vast sums of money to cause the gargantuan growth of the railroads' competition. Railroad nostalgiacs might long remember the days of the Iron Horse and of the standard Pullman, but these days are no longer here — and the transition process will continue onward.

Out of the locomotive builders shops will roll yet more powerful diesels, some equipped to run automatically, controlled by an operator hundreds of miles distant. The unit train will evolve into swift 100-mile-per-hour trains of five- and six-mile lengths capable of instantaneous loading and unloading of their commodities. The boxcar will roll off to obsolescence, with merchandise shipments being completely containerized, automatically loaded and unloaded aboard container express speedliners where they will find delivery to jet freighter aircraft such as the C5A or else loaded aboard huge ocean-going vessels. The atomic locomotive may yet become a reality. Control of the entire railroad operation may be performed by a single enormous on-line process control computer which will electronically direct all traffic movement, control all classifying operations, and produce the billing to go to the shippers of merchandise and commodities. The sleek *TurboTrain* will be the forerunner of even faster passenger hauling equipment. A system of automatically controlled commuter craft will eventually unblock the massive arterial congestion now surrounding our cities. While supersonic jetliners will shrink our planet to the size of a marble making the most distant cities only hours distant, the intercity transportation patterns will be more evenly distributed between the most optimum transportation forms, be they jet airliner, automobile, bus, or train.

This is the future. The transition we have witnessed on the railroads is but a preliminary to the even more vast transition of tomorrow. We have seen how vital the railroads have been by almost witnessing their utter collapse, and now we are witnessing their renaissance at a time when our entire national well-being depends upon them, even more so than was the case when our young nation's initial period of growth was occurring in the nineteenth century.

The challenge of the future is there. The railroads must rise to meet it, in the admirable manner they have done so far up to now.

Our nation cannot afford for them not to.

The railroaders and the carbuilders learned a lesson they would never forget from the success of the piggy-backs and the tri-level auto rack cars. No longer could the railroads offer a mode of shipping goods to which the shipper had to adapt his needs. Instead, the railroads had to offer a specialized service designed to meet the needs of the shipper and allow him to move his goods at the lowest costs possible. In the wake of this came huge 60,000 gallon tank cars, and airflow-type cars designed to load powdered or pellet material by forced air.        *(Courtesy ACF Industries, Inc.)*

*(Courtesy General American Transportation Corp.)*

Advanced concepts in unit trains were also making their way to the railroads. This articulated aluminum unit hopper car prototype has been built by Aeronca Manufacturing Corp., Middletown, Ohio, for the Southern Railway System. Fabricated from specially formed aluminum plate and extrusions supplied by Aluminum Company of America, the four-unit, eight-axle car has an over-all length of 105 feet. With unloaded weight of 40 tons, it can carry a 260-ton load. Alcoa furnished design and fabricating assistance. The car has four fast-action bottom-discharge doors in each unit. The units are coupled by pin joints, requiring only 12 inches of space. Inverted "V" transoms atop the end between units span the intervening space to permit loading from overhead hoppers while the car is moving.

(*Courtesy Aluminum Company of America*)

Nowhere was the railroads' outlook for the future more clearly indicated than in the locomotive builders' catalogs. Gone were the streamlined freight and passenger diesels. As a matter of fact, the standard-size passenger diesel was only featured as a variation of a standard general purpose model. The emphasis was on power and economy of operation.

*(All Photographs Courtesy General Motors Corp.)*

The DD-40 of General Motors was the crowning example of the emphasis on power and efficiency. The most powerful single-unit locomotive built, it packed a walloping 6000-horsepower in its elongated hood.
(*Courtesy General Motors Corp.*)

With new cars, new locomotives, new electronic controls, and hopefully a new outlook on life, the railroads of the Northeast Quadrant were facing competition squarely: to win back a goodly share of the lost freight business.

But what were the railroads doing to win back the passenger traffic that was now strangling our airways and expressways?

The French had an answer as early as 1955.

(*Courtesy French National Railroads*)

Roaring down the track faster than the camera's eye, the French locomotive CC7107 set a new world's rail speed record on March 28, 1955, when it reached the incredible speed of 205.6 miles per hour (331 km per hour). This record was matched on the following day by another French electric locomotive, the BB9004. These records were set during speed runs conducted by the French Railroads as a means of testing the effects of stress on both locomotives and track. As a result of these experiments, schedules on certain lines in France were accelerated, especially on the run of the crack "Mistral" express from Paris to the Riviera. "Le Mistral," the world's fastest train, now makes Paris–Lyon, a distance of 318 miles, in exactly 4 hours, an average speed of 79.5 miles per hour including one stop.

(*Courtesy French National Railroads*)

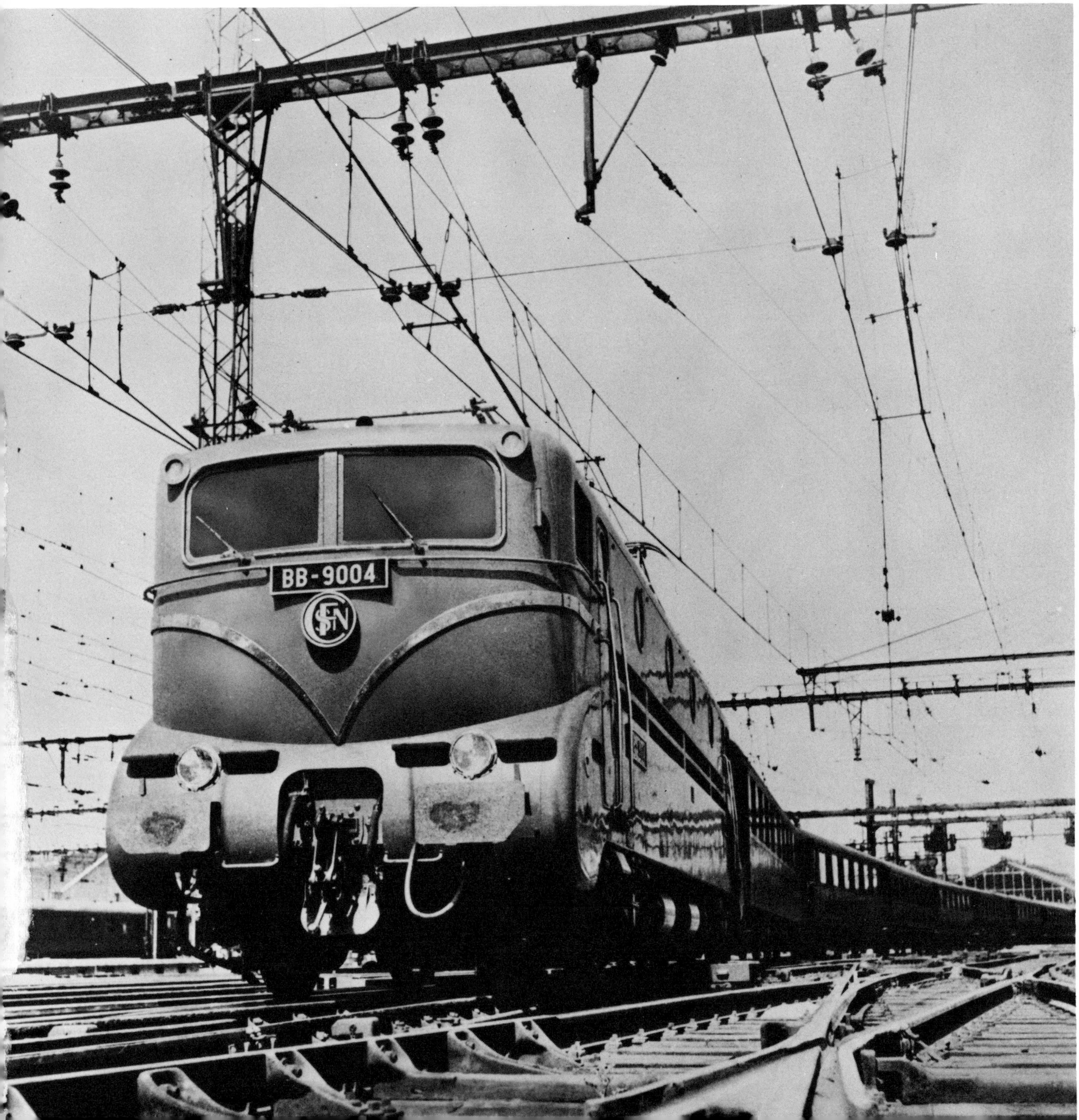

(*Courtesy Japanese National Railroads*)

230

While the French had posted the world's speed record, the Japanese were making sustained speed in intercity passenger train travel an everyday word with their New Tokaido Line featuring the bullet-nosed *Hikari* trains operating at 130 miles per hour.

From Tokyo to Osaka, a distance of 310 miles . . .

(*Courtesy Japanese National Railroads*)

. . . it took only three hours flat.

An entirely new concept of railborne transportation
had been evolved . . .

A passenger train that did not grind, rattle, squeak, or
spend everlasting hours in terminals unloading and
loading express while the passengers must wait . . .

(*Courtesy Japanese National Railways*)

. . . but instead races passengers in total comfort and total dependability to their destination. . .

The passenger train was not about to vanish from Japan . . . not at 130 mph.

But this was overseas . . . what were we doing here in America?

Four special test cars were built for the Department of Commerce by the Budd Company for the purpose of conducting high-speed tests on an improved 21-mile section of Pennsylvania Railroad track between Trenton and New Brunswick, New Jersey. In tests conducted in late spring of 1967, these cars posted a top speed of 121 miles per hour.

(*Courtesy General Electric*)

The Pennsylvania Railroad under a $90 million Federal appropriation to develop a high-speed system of intercity transport by rail had placed a $20 million order for 160 mph electric self-propelled railcars designed for service between New York and Washington.

*(Courtesy Pennsylvania Railroad)*

To be built by the Budd Company, this fleet of 50 high-speed railcars will offer the ultimate in comfort as well as 110 mph and high speeds. The interior noise is to be no greater than that of an executive office. With high-backed seats and individually controlled lighting and air-conditioning, the Budd streamliners will be a decided improvement over the conventional 50-mph passenger train.

*(Courtesy Pennsylvania Railroad)*

Meanwhile, the New York Central had also unveiled something radically new. . . . .

. . . . . a railcar with a pair of jet engines taken from an Air Force bomber and a long, sloping nose. The M-497 rolled out of the New York Central shops to prove that what the French could do in the way of speed tests with existing equipment could be performed elsewhere, as for example, on the flatlands of Ohio and Indiana.

*(Courtesy New York Central)*

It sounded like a jet approaching in the sky, to the residents living near New York Central tracks between Butler, Indiana and Stryker, Ohio. It was a jet, all right, but it wasn't in the sky. Along the high iron whooshed the M-497 like a fighter plane, leaving a solid trail of dust and trackside spectators taking cover along the way. It also left something else. . . . a new rail speed record in the United States of 183.85 miles per hour. The tests of the M-497 proved that conventional equipment and track could be used for high-speed service after all.

*(Courtesy New York Central)*

240

In Hartford, *TurboTrain* had emerged from the drawing boards . . .
*(Courtesy United Aircraft Corporate Systems Division)*

(*Courtesy of United Aircraft Corporate Systems Div.*)

. . . with the hope that this new train could revitalize . . .

...our sick transportation system...
(*Courtesy of United Aircraft Corporate Systems Div.*)

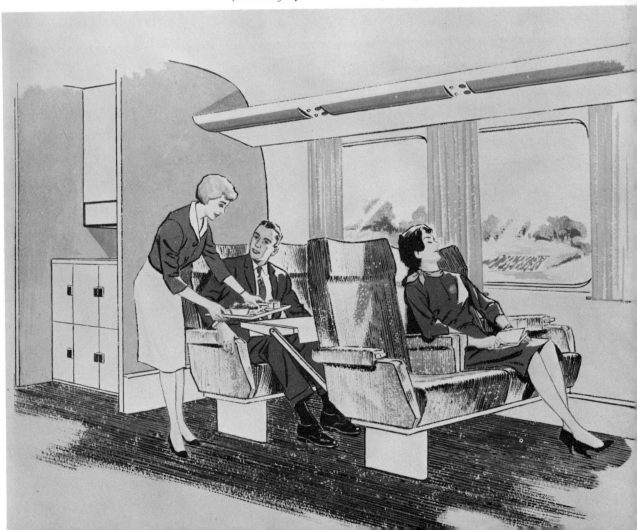

...which was congesting our highways...

244

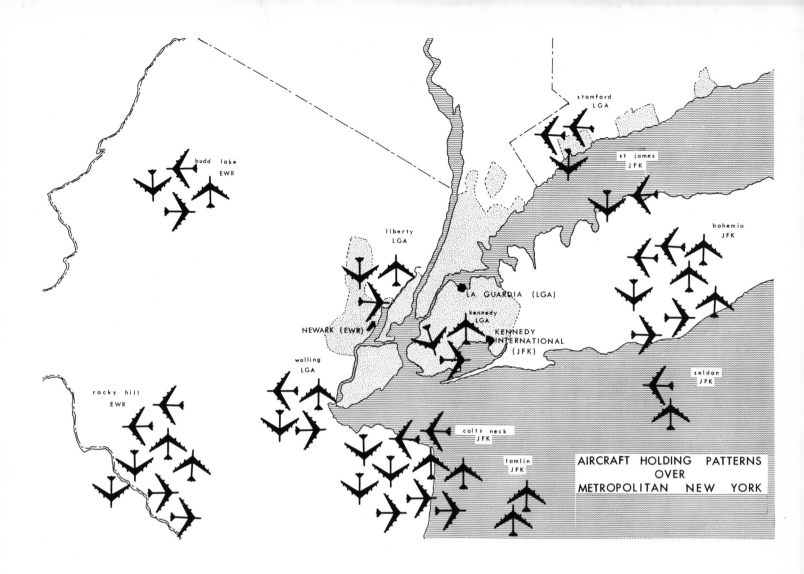

budd lake
EWR

stamford
LGA

st james
JFK

bohemia
JFK

liberty
LGA

LA GUARDIA (LGA)

NEWARK (EWR)

kennedy
LGA

KENNEDY
INTERNATIONAL
(JFK)

rocky hill
EWR

walling
LGA

seldon
JFK

colts neck
JFK

tomlin
JFK

AIRCRAFT HOLDING PATTERNS
OVER
METROPOLITAN NEW YORK

246

. . . and our skyways.

The metropolitan centers of New York and Chicago would be no more than nine hours apart via high -speed ground transport . . . and many metropolitan centers would be even closer . . .

. . . at the heart of downtown, not at a remote airport.

Intercity travel would take on an entirely new form . . .

. . . a pleasant one.

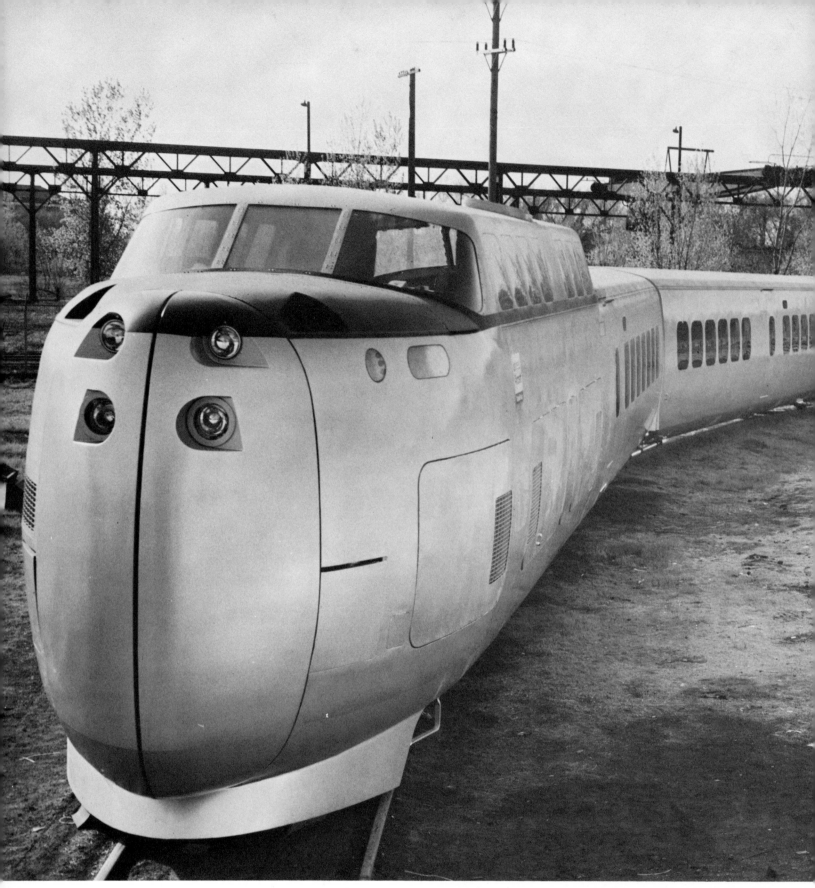

The first two TurboTrains made their appearance in the spring of 1967. In late summer, these trains will be used in demonstration revenue runs between Boston and New York, after additional testing on the high-speed test track in New Jersey. Meanwhile, a seven-car TurboTrain is due to go into service between Toronto and Montreal in late 1967, designed to provide service averaging initially 84 miles per hour. The era of the high-speed corridor train on the North American continent has thus arrived.

*(Courtesy Department of Transportation)*

As TurboTrain was making its initial appearance onto the railroad, yet another new departure from the conventional passenger train was unveiled. Designed by Sundberg-Ferar, Inc. of Detroit, the automobile-on-train concept was initiated by the Department of Transportation. The basic idea is that the entire family can ride aboard the family automobile in a specially-equipped, air-conditioned train from Washington, D.C., to Jacksonville, Florida, in restful comfort; and without incurring problems with luggage, children, or transfers can arrive at their destination in twelve hours. The Atlantic Coast Line is the participating railroad.

(*Courtesy Sundberg-Ferar, Inc.*)

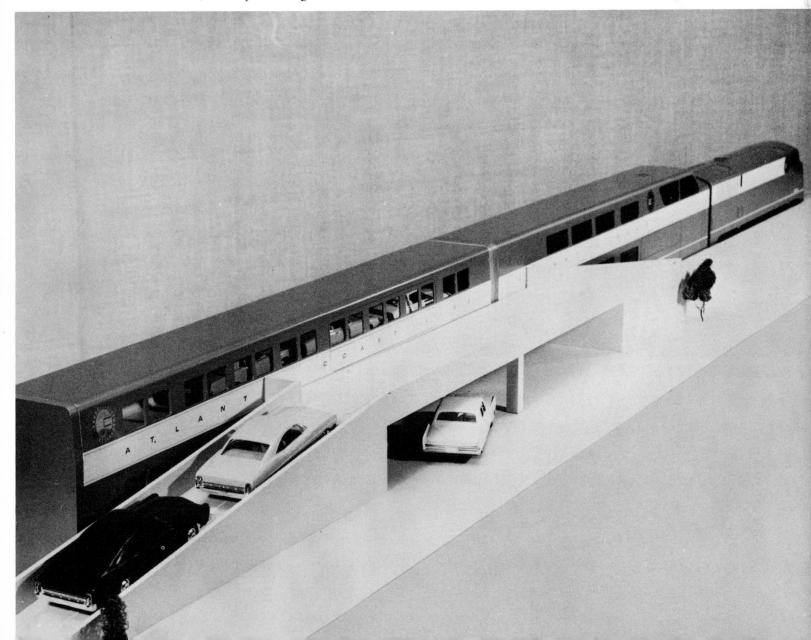

(*Courtesy Sundberg-Ferar, Inc.*)

This interior view of the lower level of a full-scale
wooden mock-up of the auto-on-train car shows the
amount of space passengers will have to leave their
autos and stroll about or walk to the lounge-and-service
cars that will be part of each train. The large windows
of the auto-on-train cars were designed to give passengers a panoramic view of the countryside.

And while the corridor trains such as TurboTrain or
the vacation-type trains such as the auto-on-train experiment are the first steps in revolutionary new pasenger
travel . . .

. . . they will not be the last, for the need for dynamic and progressive program of continuous innovation for our railroads has been demonstrated.  In the past twenty years, the railroads have undergone the greatest transition in their history, from the Iron Horse to the 160-mile-an-hour corridor train.

(*Courtesy General Electric*)

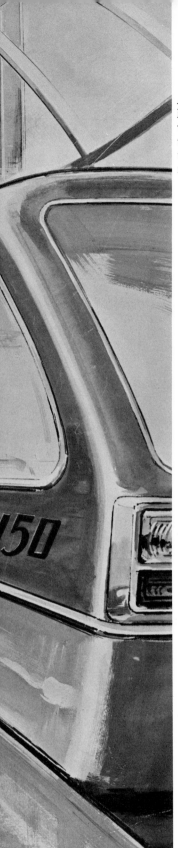

An example of railroading yet to come is a network of high speed corridor routes linking metropolitan areas with 200-mile-per-hour trains and interchanging at central stations with all other forms of ground transportation operating within the metropolitan area, such as rapid transit, bus, auto, and taxi.

The next twenty years should witness an even more astounding transition, with concepts of transportation becoming realities that now exist only in the imagination of those in our generation . . . who are entrusted with planning for the needs of generations yet to come.

(*Courtesy General Electric*)

# Index